The Art of Trial Process

Kai Yang

The Art of Trial Process

An Outline of Judicial Philosophy in China

法律出版社
LAW PRESS · CHINA

Springer

Kai Yang
Center for Rule of Law Strategy Studies
East China University of Political
Science and Law
Shanghai, China

ISBN 978-981-15-6433-8 ISBN 978-981-15-6434-5 (eBook)
https://doi.org/10.1007/978-981-15-6434-5

Jointly published with Law Press China
The print edition is not for sale in China (Mainland). Customers from China (Mainland) please order the print book from: Law Press China.

This Springer imprint is published by the registered company Springer Nature Singapore Pte Ltd.
The registered company address is: 152 Beach Road, #21-01/04 Gateway East, Singapore 189721, Singapore

Preface

The Pursuit of Truth, Goodness, Beauty and Happiness
Is the Legal Basis on Enhancing Judicial Credibility
In the Background of the New Four Modernizations

With the rapid development of the new technology revolution and the information age, today's society is undergoing profound changes, the "new four modernizations"—new industrialization, informatization, urbanization, agricultural modernization—are gradually changing the traditional ideas and the traditional mode of social production and life. To adapt to the changes of the times and social development, our traditional judicial system is also facing the deep transformation and development. In the third and fourth plenary session of the 18th Central Committee of the Communist Party of China, the party put forward that a new round of judicial reform is to actively adapt to the needs of social transformation of reality, through judicial reform and enhancing the credibility of the judiciary, realize the modernization of judicial system of governance and governance capacity. The full implementation of judicial reform initiatives, such as the quota system for judges, judicial accountability system and judicial personnel classification management, ultimately depends on the increase of overall judicial capacity and judicial level of the whole judicial professions, including quota judges, judge assistants, judicial clerks, and judicial police.

In this study, it is found that the art of adjudication of judges and other staff is actually the solid foundation for the promotion of judicial credibility under the background of the "new four modernizations". The original intention to implement reform of judicial personnel classification management, quota judge system, judicial accountability system is, through the reform of system and mechanism, to change the overpowering administrative and localization factors in operation of the traditional judicial system and mechanism, and thus to greatly enhance judicial ethics and occupation skills of the judicial occupation team—the judges, judge assistants, judicial clerks, judicial police, etc. Only if overall integral lifting of the judicial ethics and judicial professional skills of judicial professional groups, it is possible to realize the course of justice, and then to enhance the judicial credibility, and to establish the judicial authority in the whole society. Take the pursuit of truth, goodness, beauty and happiness of the judicial ethics and judicial art as the legal basis to enhance the judicial credibility, judicial adjudication can not only solve the social contradictions and disputes, but also create good public order, and then judicature will become the best governance mode ruled by law in the law-based society.

The reform of quota judge system has an important function, that is, to enhance the overall judicial ethics and trial skills of comprehensive professional judges, through the judicial system reform and the operation mechanism of adjudicative powers reform, the judicial ethics and trial skills of professional judges will be promoted to the realm of judicial art, let the judicial art become occupation realm and pursuit of the quota judges, let the judicial art become a solid foundation for improving the public credibility of the judiciary, enable the people to experience the fairness and justice in the judicial process and judgment result of each and every judicial case, make judicial reform bonus really benefit the masses of the people, let the people really feel happiness brought by the judicature and the law.

When it comes to art, people will be naturally reminiscent of beauty and happiness —the beauty of literary, the beauty of the string, the beauty of technique, the beauty of painting, the beauty of suspenseful image, the beauty of drama depicting the life, and the pleasure and joyful experience that all these many wonderful feelings bring us. Deep in people's heart, art is a kind of pure beauty, a kind of real happiness. A trade, a technique or an occupation skill of any kind, if practice makes perfect, skill goes beyond Dao, brings people the beauty and happiness, and that is art!

Is it possible for the judge's trial to become a professional art that can lead to a sense of beauty and happiness? The answer is yes! The judicial activity is a kind of legal professional work, a kind of strong practical, experiential, intellectual and technical work, the trial of a judge is not only to act like a "law crafts people", who mechanically settle disputes according to the law, but also to creatively apply the law following the spirit and principle of legislation, maintain fairness and justice of the society through judicial trial. Judge's judicial art is both the category of legal methodology, and the summary of judicial practice and trial experience. "Dismemberment of ox by Paodin" in *Chuang-tzu* is the story of judge's judicial art, the most vivid and appropriate metaphor. This story tells us about the truth of "definition", as the Chinese saying goes, every profession produces its own topmost master in all trades and processions. No matter what the industry is, practice makes perfect, skilled technology achieves the universal law. Train skills according to the law of beauty, understand the universe rules, so that people get the enjoyment of beauty, realize happy life, so all walks of life are art! There's no doubt that the judge's trial is a professional art, and it is a professional art with a great deal of knowledge!

The art of adjudication has been recognized for a long time, but at different times, people's cognitive level is different. There are many contents on the judge's judicial art in Chinese ancient legal history records: for example, since the Western Zhou Dynasty, the judicial practice of ancient China has "Five Observing" hearing ways to read people's faces, this is a trial method and technique, which is characterized by learning and grasping the parties psychological activities; as another example, in judicial practice, officials in the Song Dynasty identify the facts of the case in accordance with the law on the basis of accurately grasping the psychological activities of the parties on the one hand, and based on the actual situation of case, take poetries, stories and metaphor as examples, inspire the party's consciousness, pursue a kind of "harmony" realm combined with natural justice, national law and human feelings through the trial, shape the ideal personality under the infiltration of Chinese culture on the other hand.[1] In ancient Chinese judicial official verdicts, in addition to legal content, it is filled with humanistic emotions between the lines. Moreover, in the court verdict of the ancient scholar-officials, there are many references to poetry, music and even the flower are borrowed to describe the truth of brotherhood and moral love, to integrate law education into natural justice, human feelings and national law. For Literati in Song Dynasty, it is not an easy thing to deal with the disputes on marriage, farmland or property. Balancing the relationship among natural justice, national law and human feelings, it is an art,[2] the art of hearing a case. The beauty of prudence on accurately grasping the litigant psychological activities by the method of watching, the beauty of reason on the pursuit of harmony with emotion, reason and law in the case, the beauty of great kindness on trying to persuade human beings to realize the truth and turn towards good by allusion writing in the court verdict, are the concrete embodiments of judicial art of Chinese ancient judicial officers.

In the Republic of China, in his collection *The Art of Law* the jurist Wu Jingxiong drew the conclusion that law and judicature are art. He believed that justice is the complex of truth, goodness and beauty, and since justice is closely bound to law and judicature, law and judicature are also the complex of truth, goodness and beauty: the truth is the basis of justice, the good is the material and object of justice, and the beauty is the quality of justice. Dr. Wu Jingxiong said in his article: "When I compare law with other arts, I do not speak in a figurative or rhetorical sense. I perceive, on the one hand it is law, on the other hand it is music, poetry and painting, the two things are the same.... The means of expression, in music is sound, in poetry is word, in painting is color, when it comes to law is interest. The difference is only in the performance of the materials and media, the most important aspect of all art is the same, that is a symmetric, orderly, harmonious arrangement and the organic organization of performance elements. If the law is not art, it is nothing."[3]

---

[1]Chen [1].

[2]Chen [1].

[3]Lv [2, p. 554].

American jurist Fuller believed that legal system is a "practical art".[4] Judge Posner also mentioned that the new traditionalist opinion of anti-parsimony, "to put it another way, law is a kind of art—an art of conducting social management by law, and practicing by persons trained by law and with legal experience".[5] I think that the conclusion made by the two great jurists in the contemporary Western world leads to a proposition: judicial adjudication is a practical art!

The law does not enforce its own, the good law and system need to be realized by the judicial activities of judges. Just as without the artist's creative work, the creative idea of beauty can only be an imagination; and without the creative judicial practice of judges, the good legal system can only be a utopian dream of the legislator. The mission of judges is to apply the inherent law of the spiritual level to judicial process, and express it in reality in judicial practice.

The human beings in civilized society are not only the existence of body, but also the existence of spirit, and the nature of the inherent law of spirit is the law of beauty, the law of objectification of human essential power, the rule of human aesthetic activities. The pursuit of beauty is the concentrated reflection of humanity and human nature, is the highest human need and the limit of pursuit. Through feeling, experiencing and abstracting the truth, the good, the beauty of the object continuously, the human beings extract the elements of beauty, so that the human spirit can get eternal comfort, the human mind tends to be clear. As a social activity, judicial adjudication, should also follow the laws of beauty, reflect the humanity and human nature, and through judicial skills and techniques to balance the interests between people, to promote the expression of truth and good between people, to establish the unity of regularity and purposiveness, to realize the harmony between people in society ruled of law. Therefore, "establish and create the art of adjudication by following the laws of beauty" is a sociological proposition, it associates justice with aesthetics, looks forward to the legal professionals become the creator of the world beauty, looks forward to every case hearing by judge become art embodied of the truth, the good and the beauty, thus via the process of art creation by judicial adjudication, people can experience and feel the heart-thrilling beauty of the rule of law!

Any beautiful things are expressed in the form of formal beauty and content beauty, judge's judicial art is the unity of formal beauty and content beauty as well. Beautiful things are often with its vivid form, color, sound and body, to express people's emotional feelings, various forms of beauty in the form of natural law of extraordinary regularity (such as balance, proportion, tempo, rhythm) have become the object of beauty.[6] Although judge's judicial art does not have a gorgeous color elegant voice and distinctive appearance and other static formal beauty as calligraphy, painting, music and other artworks, it has a variety of dynamic inner beauty reflected in the minds of litigants and the public, which is far more better than other works of art in aesthetic expression. With rational-legal language used in handling

[4]Lv [3, p. 50].

[5]Lv [4, p. 553].

[6]Wang [5, p. 29].

cases, the judge shows us the beauty of linguistic rationality, which is simple and clean, concise and comprehensive; the judge presiding over the trial, accurately controlling the time, atmosphere, rhythm, timing, with which the entire trial shows us the normative beauty of orderly, smoothly, focused, and neatly. When presiding over the mediation, the judge enlightens the two parties with reason, moves them with affection, convinces them with laws, thus balances the relationship between the rights and obligations of anomie with superb mediation skills, makes the damaged personal and property relationship be clear and harmonious again, and shows us the harmonious beauty of valuing justice above material gains and advocating stability; in the process of handling cases, the judge abiding by the spirit and principle of legislation, interpreting and applying the laws creatively in order to safeguard social fairness and justice, which not only embody the beauty of morality and humanity of the judicial adjudication, but also embody the integrated beauty of the rule of law; by analyzing the law and reasoning in legal documents, the judge can convey perceptual beauty and rational beauty by the brilliant writing. In addition, judge's judicial art has more profound connotation of beauty: the spirits and principles embodied in the judicial adjudication, naturally have ingenious beauty; the judicial adjudication taking substantive fairness and procedural justice as the core, which embodies the truth, the good and the beauty of human nature; the judicial adjudication confirming human's subject status, human's dignity, value and conduct, which embodies the beauty of personality; the judicial adjudication emphasizing on the legality and continuity of the procedure, all linked with another, solid uniformed, which embodies the beauty of ups and downs and free-flowing style; the judicial adjudication taking legal thinking as the mainline, making people aware of their rights and obligations, to obtain advantages and avoid disadvantages in accordance with statutory rules, which embodies the beauty of reason; the humanity and rationality of natural order and social order reflected by the judicial adjudication, embodies the beauty of the harmony of regularity, reason and feeling, and the beauty of the union of heaven and human.

The living conditions of a nation create a unique legal system of it, but every nation always can never do without the general desire for beauty; the pursuit and competition of beautiful things, is the driving force of human progress, the meaning of human life lies in the fact that it yearns for beauty, advocates beauty, appreciates beauty, and moving forward along the direction and the imprinting of beauty. As the creator of the beauty, the judge shall stick to the laws of beauty, taking every case as beautiful flower in the garden, producing each case into a collection of art treasures in the "rule of law" museum, makes it become the interpretation and enlightenment of the goodness of humanity. Away from the law of beauty, the judicial adjudication will deviate from the long-term direction of social fairness and justice, the judge occupation will lose the social significance on maintaining the fine social order, so it is the eternal theme of the judicial adjudication to following the laws of beauty!

Advocating the value of happiness is another element of the judge's trial. In human history, the first written code of ancient Babylon "the Code of Hammurabi" pointed out at the beginning, "I established law and justice in the land and promoted the welfare of the people."[7] Although the people of different times, different stages and different ideas always have different opinions of what is "fairness" and "happiness", but who can deny this King Hammurabi's statement "is beyond all space and time, and expresses the essential value of the law spirit".[8] The essence of the spiritual value of law is the pursuit of happiness, so that the law which can make people feel happiness is a good law. If the judge's trial leads to the results of producing tyranny, suppressing kindness and filling with injustice and partiality, it is more terrible than evil! Foul examples corrupt the stream, but foul sentence or tyranny corrupt the fountain, it is the biggest evil, it is the biggest sorrow! On the contrary, if the result of the judge's trial can make people have feelings of happiness, it will be the biggest social welfare, because happiness means that law and justice have brought security, peace, equality, respect for freedom; happiness means that people can enjoy their lives in a rational society, means the realization of the legal ideals have brought the people of sincerity, kindness and beauty; means that people's interests are the most impartial secular equilibrium! Therefore, the judges must construct happiness values, with a heart of protecting people's happiness to reinterpret the purpose of trialing, following the laws of beauty, to jointly build the spiritual connotation of judicial art, and this is the soul of judicial art!

The governance of the modern state and society mainly depends on the legal tools; the process of human history has repeatedly proved that only governance by law is compatible with the development of modern society.[9] The main content of governance by law is the governance by justice, and the judge's trial is the most important content of governance by justice. The value orientation of the judge's trial largely determines whether the legal ambition and legal value can be realized. Judge Gray said, "The judge's decision is the law." The judge's trial is the process of comparing and correcting the static legal provisions with vivid and specific case facts, as well as the process of spreading and permeating the legal spirit, thus it is the practice of social governance that can best embody the legal faith. The famous ancient Greek philosopher Plato specifically discussed the importance of the judge in his masterpiece *Laws*, "Presumably it's clear to everyone that although the giving of laws is a grand deed, still, even where a city is well equipped; if the magistrates established to look after the well-formulated laws were unfit, then not only would the laws no longer be well founded, and the situation most ridiculous, but those very laws would be likely to bring the greatest harm and ruin to cities."[10] Therefore, the realization of the law value depends on the full play of the utility of the judge's profession, to a large extent the two things above are interlinked, is a dialectic unity.

From ancient to modern times, there are widely differing versions on the legal value and judicial value, the German jurist Jhering wrote in his *The Struggle for Law*, "The goal of law is peace." *The Declaration of Independence* of the United

[7]Robert [6, p. 9].

[8]Yu [7, p. 16].

[9]Cheng [8, p. 8].

[10]The Law of Plato, translated, with Notes and Interpretive Essay by Thomas L. Pangle, The University of Chicago Press, Chicago and London, p. 136.

States and *Declaration of the Rights of Man and of the Citizen* of France define the value of law as human rights and freedom. Plato interpreted the value of law as the justice of philosophers in his *The Republic*. Generally speaking, the value of law is to maintain fairness and justice, the purpose of legal governance is to maintain a stable social order, to safeguard people's lives and stability of the social environment. However, due to the different standards of fairness and justice, in the past, there have been events in which the law deviated from its true value, which means the values of law and judicature shall be refined. In my opinion, the ultimate value of law is "to make people happy"! Social fairness and justice should be arranged appropriately for the public basement on happiness, in the arrangement, people enjoy the rights under the law and undertake corresponding obligations, live together in a harmonious society full of sympathy and tenderness. The ultimate value of the judge's trial should also help the people to realize the good expectation of happiness!

The law-based governance has been fully implemented in the entire parts of constitution and laws, national governance, social governance and judicial reform, and it marks China has embarked on the journey of building a society ruled by law. When our society from the "rule of man" to "rule of law", we need not only the rule of good law, but also good judges defend the dignity of law faithfully and intelligently, and defend the fine social order established by good law. As we know, the more the rule of law has been applied, the country is stronger. Moreover, if the legal profession comes prosperous, the rule of law will be prosperous, the country is strong, only if the legal profession becomes strong; the community of judges is the faithful watcher of the law, and the main force of China advancing towards democracy and rule of law.

China has its own unique national conditions, the rule of law in China's social environment is also a special complexity, in China, implementing the rule of law, improving the judicial capacity of judges, are far more difficult than the West. Therefore, as we can imagine, how many practical difficulties the professional judges face. No matter in common law or in civil law countries, the professional ethics, skills and methods of judges have developed into an independent knowledge in the field of judicial practice and theoretical research. The judge's application of law, methods and skills of interpreting the law, and the experience of the judge's trial have been sublimated into a unique professional science after a long period of accumulation and research. It is because of the professional science, Western judges can judge right and wrong with the spirit of the law in the practice of the governance by law, the world tends to be orderly and peaceful, and people can feel the different levels of safety and happiness. In comparison, the legal education in China today has not totally researched and developed education courses on judicial ethics, judicial skills and judicial methods systematically, normatively, and scientifically, and there is no systematic, standard, occupational and professional training on legal ethics and trial of traditional art in the people's courts at all levels in China today. However, the most urgent need of the professional judges chosen from the reform of quota judge system is the professional ethics, professional skills and judicial art. Moreover, the quota judges chosen by a new round of judicial reform not only need to master general skills and methods of legal interpretation and legal application, but also need to develop the judicial occupation ethics, and have a higher level of judicial art! The ideal state of judicial art is to convey the truth, kindness and beauty of the law to people, to achieve harmonious and safe judicial social governance under the background of "the new four modernizations"; at the same time, also means that our legal professional community can treat noble and sacred judicial power seriously, exercise adjudication according to the law of truth, goodness and beauty, safeguard the equality and freedom of the people, and carry out the happiness and Great Harmony for our society!

Tracking back the history, again, let us review the oath in the Code of Hammurabi, the first written code in human history, "I established law and justice in the land and promoted the welfare of the people." This voice is the most profound understanding of the human spirit of all laws! The enlightenment to us is, the judge's trail should pay attention to social life, sympathize with people's feelings, in order to realize the value pursuit of truth, goodness, beauty and happiness, thus create the judicial art. This will be the ideal realm and spiritual pursuit of the professional community of quota judges for the whole life.

Shanghai, China Kai Yang
June 2020

References

1. Chen J (1997) On the principle of virtue and the art of trial in the judicial activities of the literati and officialdom in the song dynasty—A study on chinese traditional legal culture II, Law Science, Sixth
2. Lv S (2004) The truth, goodness and beauty of law–Primary exploration of legal aesthetics, Law Press China, p 554
3. Lv S (1997) Study on contemporary western jurisprudence, China Renmin University Press, p 50
4. Lv S (2004) The truth, goodness and beauty of law–Primary exploration of legal aesthetics, Law Press China, p 553
5. Wang C (1981) Aesthetics illuminated, People's Publishing House, p 29
6. Robert F H (1904) The code of Hammurabi–King of Babylon, The University of Chicago Press, p 9
7. Yu D (2004) Searching for the law's trail, Law Press China, p 16
8. Cheng Z (2001) The judicial reform and the politics development, China Social Sciences Press, p 8

Contents

Chapter 1
A General View on the Chinese Judges' Judicial Art

In the art of law, judges should be interpreted as artists. The real law cannot be found in the books of laws and regulations, but in the interpretation of the judge, because, as music is not something in music book, law is not in the book.
—Wu Jingxiong, The Art of Law

Art is universal. Art is not bound to any particular country or to any particular period of time. For art is as old as human race, and it is just as much part of man as are his eyes or his ears or his hunger or his thirst.
—Hendrik Willem Van Loon, The Arts of Mankind

1 The Art of Adjudication is a Professional Art

When it comes to art, firstly people would ask what is art? How to define the concept of art? To give a precise definition of art is very difficult, because art is a constantly changing and developing concept, it has a very distinctive character of the time, along with the time development and social progress, the connotation of the concept of art is also expanding. First of all, let's try to understand and comprehend the concept and the essence of art from a variety of different points of view.

It has been said that art is a reflection of social life; some people think that art is the expression of the author's mind, art is the aesthetic ideology. In any case, art is the product of human creation as subject, the production of any artworks must go through a process from the author to the works then to the audience on the basis of life. If define the concept of art from the essence of art, art has a narrow interpretation (only including visual and auditory art), broad interpretation (narrow sense of art and literature), generalized interpretation (including all kinds of beautiful utility products, such as a fighter, a teacup), etc., to define the connotation of art from the distinction between art and non-art, art is a kind of cultural form with practical spirit, is a kind of ideology which is free from the economic base, is a concentrated aesthetic form.[1] The Soviet esthetician Pelov pointed out three kinds of arts: the first one is

[1]Li [1], pp. 6–72.

Y. Kai, *The Art of Trial Process*,
https://doi.org/10.1007/978-981-15-6434-5_1

the broadest sense of art, "means any kind of skill", "this is cleverly, sophisticatedly, skillfully completing the task people proposed in production, organization, ideology and other activities. It can be skilled in coal mining, planting wheat, driving trains and managing factories, building houses and writing poems, pulling out sick teeth and forecasting the weather, making math and playing football". The concept of "art" here is actually a reference to a skill that is completely different from the purely aesthetic point of view. The second one refers to the creations of "according to the laws of beauty", which are divided into two categories: one belongs to the field of material civilization. This is something that is used in social and private life, for people's material requirements, while at the same time created in accordance with the laws of beauty, such as clothing, furniture, utensils, etc. Another one belongs to the human spiritual civilization, refers to the original meaning of "artistic creation", such as painting, sculpture, architecture, literature art, music and drama, this can be specially separated as the third meanings of art, which is the narrowest sense of art, and the art as the object of the research and discussion in general philosophy of art and the theory of art.[2] Ueda Min, a Japanese scholar, said: "the ideas contained in art cannot be written in the language of intelligence. Once it is written down, the weight of the original would be reduced. As teaching poems, some people would often heckle: "the meaning of this poem, in a nutshell a word, what is it?" But this is impossible to tell in a word in any case." Art connotation performs a thought, unknown, partly appearing partly disappearing, to support philosophy and science, it is the generalized "art".[3] French scholar Danner believes that the purpose of art is to show the main characteristics of things, to show the prominent and significant attributes of things, an important point of view, a major state. When people present basic reason and basic law in art, they won't use the boring definition which can only be understood by the experts instead of the public, but use the easy ways to feel, not only appeal to the intellect, but also appeal to sense and emotion of the ordinary people. Art has a characteristic, which is "high and popular" things, convey the most advanced content to the public.[4] In Van Loon's words, art is universal. Art is not bound to any particular country or to any particular period of time. For art is as old as human race, and it is just as much part of man as are his eyes or his ears or his hunger or his thirst.[5]

We believe that the concept of art should fully express its meaning: art is mainly for occupation, job or work, its subject is human, its object is the psychology, emotion and cognition of human, as well as the relationships among human beings. Art should be defined as a concept closely related to occupation or work, art refers to the experience, wisdom, courage, inspiration, strategy, creative and comprehensive ability of the subject in occupation and work, perform creative play and prospect, its manifestation is the creative use of various occupation skills and techniques to achieve reach the level of skillful or a realm of freely use, and make people have a

---

[2]Chen [2], pp. 1–2.

[3]Ueda [3], p. 47.

[4]Taine [4], pp. 34–62.

[5]Hendrik [5], p. 23.

sense of beauty. "Chuang-tzu" mentioned in the two stories of "Dismemberment of ox by Paodin" and "Cutting wood for wheels by Lunbian" are about the most vivid example of the concept of art.

If art is connected with the adjudication of judges, it is necessary to understand and acknowledge the judges' professional background. The legal profession is a highly practical occupation, which requires both profound legal knowledge and the accumulation of professional experience and the experience of social life. The judge's adjudication activity is closely related to the experience of the judicial trial and the social life, the occupation emphasizes that the judges should be trained and cultivated for a long time. From the view of jurisprudence, the truth, kindness and beauty of law should be reflected and displayed by judges with superior judgment art in specific cases in judicial practice. The rule of law is a lofty ideal, but because of the impossibility and the imperfect of the rule of law, the rule of law is always the human desire and direction, thus the rule of law is an eternal process, is a kind of state not fully adapt to, which determines that it is necessary and possible to make the judicial adjudication artistic forever.

According to the provisions of the criminal law, scholars have combined with the use of computer technology to create computer sentencing software, but the computer program were ignoring the case's circumstance character, diminishing the character of emotional and reasonable of law, only can be regard as a reference for judges. Out of concern for the injustice of the judge's trial, people have also been dreamed of designing the judicial trial as a vending machine, while input facts and evidence, output a fair verdict from the vending machine. This is forever an adult fairy tale. It turns out that computers are no substitute for the human brain, which is the fundamental reason why our society still needs judges, the judicial expertise. In the society ruled by law, the judge is the guardian of the legal rules, and the practitioner of the legal rules, the judge should be a professional templars with strong sense of the main body, skilled judicial skills and techniques. The judge implements the laws and protects human rights by wisdom and conscience actively, and has an artistic quality surpass particular modes, which is beyond any mechanical power.

Here, we can conclude that judge's trial art is such kind of art: while performing judicial function, a judge comprehends and interprets the spirit of law, legislative purpose and principles correctly, in accordance with the laws of beauty and happiness values, in accordance with the circumstances of the case, determines the skills and methods of hearing the case, such as guiding principle, strategy, focus, etc., applies the best legal norms, decides the case impartially. The art of judge is a comprehensive reflection and application of moral character, personality, ability, knowledge, wisdom, inspiration and judicial experience of professional judges, we should say judges' judicial art is the universal pursuit of professional judges.

Judge Cardozo highly praised judge Holmes' adjudicature art in his article *Mr. Justice Holmes*.[6] Historian Mr. Justice Holmes is a historian and scholar, a master of the learning of the law and of its traditional technique. At every step of the way, in the smallest and greatest work, you will find legal wisdom that fits with your mission. It is, however, a knowledge of the application of law, a knowledge that has

---

[6]Cardozo [6], pp. 682–692.

been conquered, utilized, and served in philosophy. He may be groping for things vanished. He gives us glimpses of the things eternal. There are rifts in the common air that reveal an aether more luminous in the unmeasured depths beyond. Who else has been able to pack a whole philosophy of legal method into a fragment of a paragraph...As historian and mere technician his place would be secure in any survey of the legal scene.[7] Dr. Wu Jingxiong highly praised Holmes' adjudicature art: "Justice Holmes' thought is profound, he's rich in experience, knowledgeable. He has a sense of wonder about life and universe, and he believes that there are too many subtle things behind us, that the law is a natural fact, and shares the mystery of existence with other natural facts. What influences a judge to decide the case is often the calls from the depths of the universe. Holmes said, in the process of law, there are always some faint unknown part, disembodied, too fuzzy to be noticed, too symbolic to explain. Not only did he pay attention to the balance of interests, but in fact he tried to put the limited into the infinite, trying to see the infinite in the limited. These cannot be grasped by logical thinking, but must resort to emotional, this mysterious, infinite echo, this big glance cannot touch the operation process of this review, this boundless universe in the heart gently marks, isn't this the aesthetic realm?"[8] Justice Holmes' adjudicature art lies in his understanding of the legal methods, he said: "The felt necessities of the time, the prevalent moral and political theories, intuitions of public policy, avowed or un-conscious, even the prejudices which judges share with their fellow-men, have had a good deal more to do than the syllogism in determining the rules by which men should be governed. The law embodies the story of a nation's development through many centuries, and it cannot be dealt with as if it contained only the axioms and corollaries of a book of mathematics"[9] Mr. Justice Holmes' profound understanding of the legal method gives us a new enlightenment to the professional judge. Though Dr. Wu Jingxiong and Justice Cardozo's formulation on Holmes' adjudicature art, we should have a more intuitive, more emotional and more appropriate understanding and comprehension—judges' judicial art is the art of practice, is the art of method, the art of thinking!

Some may ask, why do we particularly expect judges to reach the artistic level? Is it only in the pursuit of a concept of fashion? The answer is not as simple. The ideal expectation of judges is not to decorate the hall of the rule of law, but to reach the other side of truth. As Gadamer said, art is an excellent way to reveal the truth, art is "certainly different from that sensory knowledge which provides science with the ultimate data from which it constructs the knowledge of nature, and certainly different from all moral rational knowledge, and indeed from all conceptual knowledge—but still knowledge, i.e., conveying truth".[10] The judge makes hearing cases as a profession, by handling the case in the process of long-term, the judge's judicial art is the judicial skills and techniques created and summarized by professional judges

[7] Cardozo [7], pp. 682–684.

[8] Lv [8], p. 555.

[9] Cardozo [9], p. 683.

[10] Gadamer [10], p. 84.

through learning, training, researching and exploring, It is the long-term accumulation and sublimation of the judicial practice experience, it is the highly integration of legal theory, the modern judicial philosophy, legal way of thinking, judgment skills and techniques, trial experience, social experience, intuition and inspiration, the concept of legal culture, social and literary and aesthetic ability, moral values and legal values of professional judges, the purpose of judging is to reveal truth and justice, to accomplish self-confidence, trust of others, and credibility. Therefore, the purpose of raising the standard of judge's trial to the artistic level, is to promote the judges seriously considering a great aesthetic value may be proved by the adjudicature, and they may cherish their occupation honor, and understand the legal profession from the practical level to the ideal level.

There is a close relationship between the judge's judicial art and the judge's occupation. The judge is the subject of judge's judicial art, the object is the axiom, the emotion and the knowledge on judicial adjudication and legal spirit of the judges, the parties and the public.

The judge profession needs rational support of legal science knowledge, and the sensual assistant of professional skills and experience, such as judicial skills and techniques and experienced, thus using rational legal science into judicial practice, adjusting various disputes in social life by means of law, maintaining social order, safeguarding social fairness and justice. This practical process is both the process of rational practice, and the perceptual practice process beyond reason based on reason; both a process with a legal procedure and transparent implementation to realizing justice, and a process of spiritual perception for judge to conduct free evaluation, moral judgment, value choice, interest measure. Therefore, we believe that the judicial process is not only a rational scientific judgment process, but also a perceptual art creation process, permeated with rich legal connotation. We look up at Justice Holmes' consummate judicial art, feel his ingeniousness of combination of legal knowledge, statesmanship, literary quality and philosophical thinking, admire his noble realm of being keen to capture the secrets of the universe, use for judicial justice and for the benefit of society. While admiring the judge artist, should we see China's professional judges of the goals and direction? As long as taking professional training and long-term self-cultivation in the trial practice, our professional judges should also be able to become one.

2 Contents of the Art of Adjudication

After we have a general understanding of the concept and the nature of the judge's judicial art, we need to know what the specific contents of the judge's judicial art.

The judge's judicial art reflects in the whole process of judicial adjudication, mainly including: psychology art, expression art, the art of conducting oneself in society, litigation registration techniques and skills, controlling court ability and art, art of lawsuit mediation, art of interpreting laws, art of writing judgment documents, art of legal communication and researching, art of enforcing judgment, etc.

I. Judge's Psychological Art

The psychological art of judge's trial refers to a kind of trial skill in which the judge decides the corresponding trial countermeasures according to the different litigants and the different psychological activities of these litigants in the process of trial and makes the trial proceed smoothly according to the legal procedure. Judicial work is mainly the work of carrying out on human, the litigation activities are mainly carried out around the interests of people, all litigation activities are in a certain psychological context. For the parties involved in litigation, the psychological background is the psychological entanglement of the litigation, which is the sum of the psychological connection and the psychological conflict which revolve around the claim and the purpose of the action. The litigation psychological entanglement includes the contradiction and conflict between the parties in the lawsuit, the mutual exclusion in the rights and interests, and the sharp opposition of the emotion. Most of the participants in litigation activities are people with the spirit and the ability of activity, there are general rules of psychological activities, have this or that kind of psychological factors in it, these psychological factors determines the internal psychological attitude and external behavior of the litigants in the lawsuit process of to a great extent. The judge should learn and use the psychological tactics and skills right, in judicial activities, according to the psychological status of the litigant, analyze the party's litigation motivation, calculate the cost of litigation, understand master mentality, pay attention to using the right guiding ideology to guide the litigation to the balance and equilibrium of interests. On the one hand, pay attention to grasp the subjective mental state of the litigant, through effective strategies and impose psychological impact on the parties, promote the parties to produce a good psychological reaction, so as to promote the adjudication's benign operation and high efficiency; on the other hand, pay attention to the training of judges' fine psychological quality, promote all kinds of judicial trial skills and techniques to work well by improving their psychological quality. Therefore, the judge's judicial art is psychological art to a great extent. When judges with rich trial experience say "handle complicated matters with ease" in civil cases, they actually mean the grasp and use of psychological tactics in civil trial.

II. Judge's expression art

The expression art of judge's trial, that is, the techniques and skills of language and eloquence, mainly involves the two borderline jurisprudence of legal linguistics and judicial eloquence, which is an important aspect to improve the judge's trial ability. There is a very close relationship between law and language, and there is a national inalienability between the language of the judicial trial and the text form and the language of the sound form. Judge's trial cannot be separated from language and eloquence. It is very important in the quality of trial whether the judge can use the language artistically in the process of adjudication. As a professional judge, if you do not have a good language skills, or do not know how to learn the essentials and skills of judicial eloquence, you would be painful like a bird with folded wings that cannot fly in the sky. To improve the judicial eloquence of the judge, puts forward a very high request to judge culture and language ability, asks the judge to continue to improve the observation and memory ability, logical thinking ability, psychological adaptability, language control ability and face strain ability in order to enhance the judge's ability to express the law. A judge who is concerned with language arts is bound to be able to adjust the content and expression of the language according to the different characteristics of the different stages of the trial and the different rhetoric objects in the process of the adjudication, and always maintain the language norm and the decent characteristics, and reflect the respect on the equal treatment of parties' litigation rights in judicial trial.

III. Judges' humanness art

As the old saying goes, "be a decent person first, then learn how to do things", the same emphasis on the judicial art of conducting oneself in society. The judge must deal with all sorts of litigation parties every day and must deal with all aspects of the secular society. The foreign judicial system emphasizes that judges should reach a considerable age, because they believe that judges must have a certain social life experiences, and these experiences include the world of knowledge and art of conducting oneself in society.

Judges are ordinary people, also living in the secular real society which is bound to be inextricably linked with the individual and the collective in society, judge handling the case also is bound to contact and communicate with the parties of different classes. In such a human society of China, it is more difficult for judges to follow the standards of the West and to be judges who are cautious and isolated. Since living in the real world, a variety of complex social relations and the ways of the world at all times putting the judge profession on the principles and conduct to a severe test and challenge. In addition to the deep legal knowledge, sophisticated trial skills and techniques, the judge must learn to conduct himself/herself in society, must understand a certain social etiquette and social life rules, which is an important part of the judge's trial art.

In the meantime, the judge's judicial process is also a process of educating the parties and other litigation participants how to behave. The adjudication process contains many of the truth and art on "behaving", only the first to be a "human", on this basis to be a "judge". No matter how strong the judicial ability, how smart, competent, how high education, if the judge doesn't know to behave, the actual effect of the case is always questionable. Therefore, in the judge's career, how to be a human being, how to be a person who commensurate with the professional requirements of the judge, to be a popular and respected person, how to realize their career through their own personal charisma, is worthy of every judge to think through. In order to improve the professional skills of judges, to survive and develop in today's increasingly complex social environment, to adhere to the legal faith and professional ethics in front of the seduce of all kinds of interests, it is necessary to know well of "how to behave"; to improve the professional skills of judges, in order to, in the cut, the chaos of human settlements adhere to the judge's professional ethics, in the interests of various interests in front of the law faith and professional conduct, it must be well versed in "life" of the road; otherwise, our professional skills and techniques can be "proposed", it is difficult to achieve the beautiful realm of art.

The art of conducting of oneself in society includes, the performance art of dealing with people in the secular life, the cooperative art of getting along with colleagues in daily work, the communication art of recepting the parties, the adjusting art of controlling their own emotions, the rejecting art of refusing various temptations in the judicial process, the integration art of adjusting the relationship between the parties, and so on. The art of conducting of oneself for judges does not require them to be sophisticated, resourceful, and even give up their principle, but for the characteristics of the judges and the actual situation of the social environment, requires them to be a magnanimous man and work hard while handling the cases. The judge should be kind rather than obscene, sincere rather than hypocritical, warm rather than frivolous, tolerant rather than jealousy, make the following real: neither riches nor honours can corrupt him; neither poverty nor humbleness can make him swerve from principle; and neither threats nor forces can subdue him. If our judges master and use the art of behaving in the judicial process, we can set up a bridge of mutual understanding and trust between people, so as to improve the judicial image, establish judicial authority, and make greater contribution to the harmonious society through judicial adjudication.

IV. Judge registration Art

Perhaps a lot of judges and litigants do not treat the court's case filing tribunal as a purely adjudication apartment, but mistakenly thought that the business nature of the registration work was not as professional as other tribunals, and even that the registration work isn't an adjudication work. This view is completely erroneous. The adjudication character of the case filing tribunal is very strong, is the primary part of the trial work, since the level of registration work even determines the quality on the quality, level and efficiency of the entire trial activities, we can even regard the register work as the basis or premise of the judge's trial.

The court's power to judge is a passive power, according to the parties' request to start the proceedings, what judicial power started first by the parties is the power to register examination. In the context of realistic judicial power, in the context of realistic political, economic, cultural and social structures, in the realistic enforcing environment, which cases the courts can accept and which cases the courts are inadmissible; which cases should seize the best time to resolve disputes, and which cases need to go through the passage of time by "cold treatment"; which cases can be a lawsuit, and which cases do not have the conditions for filing acceptance; which cases can be solved faster and more economically by alternative dispute resolution mechanisms, and which cases can be solved by the pre litigation mediation or mediation before the court, without wasting more litigation costs and judicial resources; which disputes may cause conflicts in the trial work, which disputes may cause potential crisis... These are the problems that should be fully considered and reviewed in the register examination work. It can be said that the register examination of the case is a pre-trial and preliminary examination of the case, just like the prelude and overture to the movement. With the good start of the case, the judge's trial can be carried out smoothly. In particular, the register examination work of the grassroots courts and the basic tribunals are of great importance to the overall judicial work.

Therefore, the technique and method of register is an important part of the judge's judicial skills and techniques, and we must have the correct understanding and attitude. The skills and techniques of the register include: the skills to review the relevant legal instruments of the parties, the techniques of recepting the parties, the manner in answering questions, the techniques of pre-litigation preservation, the techniques of implementing of pre-litigation preservation, pre-execution and other coercive measures, the techniques of ascertaining jurisdiction, the techniques of preventing conflicts and resolve the potential contradictions, the techniques of registrating civil litigation, the techniques of registrating administrative litigation, the techniques of registrating criminal litigation, the techniques of registrating private prosecution, and so on.

V. The art of holding court sessions

The ability to hold court sessions is an important judicial ability, one of the necessary skills of judges, an important part of the judge's judicial art. Once upon a time, when I worked in the basic people's court, there was a classic conversation between a judge's child and the other two children: a child said, "My father is a teacher, who teaches you knowledge." Another child said, "My father is a policeman, who arrests the bad guys." The judge's child hesitated for a moment and said, "My father holds court sessions." With the simple the child's observation on the professional nature of his father, we can realize the importance of holding court sessions in the judge's profession. Holding a court session to hear a case is an important way for the people's court to exercise its jurisdiction and to fulfill the sacred duty of the Constitution to protect the legitimate rights and interests of citizens. The exercise of the judicial power independently according to law is the power and duty conferred on the judge by the Constitution and the law. Court hearing is the main position for the judge to show his talent, and it is the basic method for the judge to deal with all kinds of disputes legally, correctly, and properly. Only after holding a court session can the judge to identify the facts of the case, to determine the attribution of responsibility during the hearing, accordingly, accurately to interpret and apply the law. If compare a court to a small theater, the judge is the director and the host of the play, in the control of the judge, scenes of tragicomedies in the theater become tearful, touching legal art works. The techniques and skills of holding court sessions are the main contents of the judge's professional competence, are the integration skills of many comprehensive qualities and abilities, including: the ability to prepare before the court, the ability to organize the trial, the ability of logical thinking and judgment, the ability to summarize the contents of the trial, the ability to coordinate and mediate. Whether the judge makes it simple and clear while organizing a court session, whether the idea is clear, whether the judge can determine the facts accurately by the court session, or resolve the dispute in court, all depends on the use of the techniques and skills of controlling and directing litigation for the judge.

As the old saying goes, "Grinding a chopper will not hold up the work of cutting firewood." Preparatory work before the trial is one of the basic work of the trial. Trial reform experiences and lessons told us that the preparatory work before the trial is a crucial part of the trial, and an integral part of the whole trial. The art of war tells us that "Fight no battle unprepared; fight no battle you are not sure of winning." Preparedness ensures success, and unpreparedness spells failure. Preparatory work before the trial just like the elaborate rehearsal before a good show, carefully preparing props clothing, makeup, test stage lighting, sound effects and other necessary preparations, is the necessary preparation for the success of the performance, without these preparations, the show will not succeed. Different from the thermal field of theatrical performances, the pre-court preparation also includes the judge's prediction of the whole trial orientation and the psychological preparation of the possible events. The foundation of holding court sessions lies on the judge's understanding and grasping of the judicial proceedings. On the basis of the full understanding of the legislative intent, the judge takes corresponding measures to reflect the art of trial according to the specific circumstances of the case.[11]

We define the holding court session of judge as a form of art, not because the main way to hear the case for the professional judge is holding a court session, but because the trial techniques and skills shown by the professional judge in each court session, and law literacy of long-term application, cultural heritage and the inspiration, wisdom, creativity of the judge which can produce the beauty of art, there may be infinite aftertaste. We can find it in films and TV shows, in literary works, in historical records, and even in real life, that the wonderful court scene, the judges just like general commanders, commanding the armies, calmly, having the faith to win, showing us the great technology of controlling; or like TV presenters, adapting to guide the litigant parties debate, about right and wrong, about justice and fairness, showing us the capacity to host; or like philosopher full of wisdom and rational, distinguishing true and false, good and evil, reflecting the wisdom of speculative and judging art of the wise person in the trial process. Therefore, the ability to control the hearing is a perfect way to show the judicial occupation skill and talent of the occupation art for judges in the trial process, thus is essential technique, required course, necessary skill for judges to be competent in their lofty judicial profession.

VI. The Mediation Art

For thousands of years, in Chinese society with the Confucian tradition, both civil mediation and official mediation are very important social dispute resolution mechanisms. Mediation is one of the indispensable ways in maintaining social stability and resolving conflicts of interest. After the founding of People's Republic of China, more than 20 years of civil trial practice, under the guidance of the "Ma Xi-wu trial mode", the broad masses of professional judges actively explore the litigation

[11] Huang [11].

mediation model to mediate a large number of civil disputes, creating a lot classic mediation cases; many professional judges' mediation techniques and skills have reached high level, and brought up a large number of mediation experts. Even more, mediation is a basic principle of civil action in our country. Before the 1990s, civil cases' mediation rate has been relatively high. Since the early 1990s, the trial has entered a comprehensive reform stage, since then Chinese judges have some deviation in the understanding of the function and value of the court mediation, mediation was long-term neglected. In the folk memory, mediation seemed to be in a state of dormancy. However, the loss of the way and means of mediation, judicial trial seems to be more and more powerless in regulating social disputes. Verdict only, even substantive justice verdict, is not necessarily a good solution to the dispute, even more some may intensify social contradictions. In confusion, people began to reflect back, the courts, the society and the academic circles have begun to re-evaluate the value and function of litigation mediation, the mediation slowly revived in the folk memory.

June 13, 2002, "Legal Daily" published an article, "How the contradictions are intensified", reported the serious murder in 2001, which shocked the whole country and occurred in a large village of Daxiakou, Yuci District, Jinzhong City, Shanxi Province. Hu Wenhai, who made the great murder, was also a victim himself. He kept reporting and petitioning, and finally, because of having no recourse, he took the risk of retaliation, causing 14 people's deaths in the human. I can't help thinking that, this was supposed to be a civil dispute case which could be resolved through mediation, but because it didn't get timely and effective mediation, it led to 14 tragic deaths. Although Hu Wenhai has been severely punished by law, many of the social problems reflected exposed by the tragedy worthy of our deep reflection. Whether social dispute can be resolved by a verdict only? Whether our society needs mediation any more? How does court mediation and civil mediation play their functions in building a harmonious society? It is necessary to combine with the reform, the improvement and the development of mediation system to answer these questions.

The traditional court mediation system is now in a very awkward development dilemma, but the reality of social development calls for the evolution and renewal of the mediation system. We believe that the reform of the mediation system first lies in the change of judge group's ideas. The regeneration of the mediation system depends on the degree of emphasis on the mediation mechanism in the litigation of the professional judges, depends on the combination of the modern judicial idea and the mediation skills, and depends on the exhibition and sublimation of the mediation art of the professional judges. Applying Chinese-style political discourse, the political significance of mediation is to properly solve the "contradictions among the people", and its social significance lies in "maintaining social stability". On the micro level, mediation is an art which combines emotion, reason and law, "turning hostility into friendship"; on the macro level, mediation can be called the governance way of "rule by law" and "rule by virtue" of harmony and unity.[12] Mediation is the trial art that judges use the legal rules to resolve conflicts and disputes in the stalemate. It is an important professional technique and skill to solve social disputes during the social

[12]Liu [12], p. 105.

transformation period. The judge mediation art content is rich and profound, it's necessary for us to explore and summarize in judicial practice, especially to inject modern judicial ideas and the spirit of law in the traditional mediation system, so that the traditional mediation skills can fit modern social needs. We summarize and sublimate the mediation experience of the judge to the level of behavioral art of preventing litigation, turn the wisdom, creativity of professional judges group into vocational techniques and skills, so that litigation mediation can really become a trial art with harmonious beauty.

VII. The judgements-writing art

The openness of the trial should be fully disclosed, from the courtroom to the text of the carrier, the openness of judgements and verdicts should be contained in the openness of the trial.[13] The judgements and verdicts are the text carrier of the judicial justice, and writing judgements and verdicts is the necessary professional skill for professional judges. Like the openness of trial process, the openness of judgements and verdicts gives a way to show the judgements-writing art of Chinese judges.

To assess a judge's professional skills, there are two skills can be listed in the specific assessment criteria, one is court session, the other is judgements and verdicts. In a sense, a court session is only to provide a platform space in a background of the proceedings in order to ascertain the facts and verify the evidence, whereas refer to the decisive parts of the proceedings in hearing cases, such as "applying the laws" and "making decisions", most of them are taken place outside the court session, and characterized by the text of judgements and verdict.[14] Therefore, a part of the judicial art is reflected in the court sessions, and the other in the judgment documents. Whether the judge can produce a high-quality judgment document, which is thorough reasoning and rigorous, and in which the facts are clear and the laws are correctly interpreted, is an important criterion for measuring the level of a judge's trial, and it is one of the important contents of the judge's judicial art.

The judgment documents is the authoritative written conclusion of the judge's right to exercise the judicial power represent the country, including judgements, verdicts and mediation agreements. The practical significance of the judgment documents lies in activating the "law on paper" into the "living law" to solve the real dispute through the full "reasoning". In Anglo-American common law countries, judicial decisions of the courts can often become binding precedent and become a source of law. Some of the judgements made by famous judges in foreign countries are like high-quality papers, informative and full of jurisprudence insight, the US Supreme Court's verdict even become an important source of new ideas in jurisprudence. In contrast, the Chinese court's judgment documents are more like official documents rather than legal instruments, lack of reasoning, which is a common weakness of the Chinese judgment documents.[15] It is the only way for the professional

[13]Liu [12], p. 105.
[14]Liu [13], p. 106.
[15]Liu [13], p. 106.

judge of China to improve the judging level by writing better judgment documents, the ability in writing judgment documents should be an important indicator of the judge's vocational skills assessment. Compared with our new understanding of the reform of the judgment documents, we have a lot of room for the improvement of the writing of the judgment documents, which requires us to enrich the judgment's reasons.

The reason is the spirit and soul of the judgment, the judgment without reasoning means that the judge understands the legal theory superficially and is unable to use the legal theory to interpret the law properly; it is the tragedy of the judges' profession that the judge can't illustrate the legal basis of the decision in the judgment document. In the text of the judgment documents, which best demonstrates the theoretical foundation and the creative ability of the judge,[16] which expresses the judge's legal thoughts, the judge should make the light of wisdom shining for good. A good judgment, a judgment full of jurisprudence, human feelings, and ethics, should be able to satisfy the winning party, also convince the losing party.

We believe that the judge is using the trail art to metamorphose the universal and abstract laws into behavioral rules which are applicable to specific cases, full of life and vigour. This artistic process, in which the combination of rationality and sensibility, the integration of the subjective and objective, is embodied in the judgment documents. The judgment document is another stage for judges in addition to the court session. If the judges' professional techniques and skills can be called the judicial art, then we have reason to treat the judgment documents as legal art treasures created by professional judges. Through the judgment document created by a professional judge, the artistic form in which the legal profession interprets the laws, the professional judge clarifies the question of "what" and "why", and thus realize the purpose of resolving doubts, it is able to restore the conflicting and imbalanced states to an orderly and harmonious one, to quell the social contradictions, and to establish the belief in law and the authority of rule of law. If we have clear and thorough understanding of the characteristics of the judge occupation, we will absolutely look forward to what kind of art treasures the professional judge group would create, and be marveled by wisdom and profound thought of the judges.

Therefore, the judgment writing is an important part of the judge's judicial art, in which requires the professional judges to thoroughly understand and analyze social phenomena and legal phenomena, creative thinking, and to show complex thinking of independent character on the basis of legal thinking, including political thinking, economic thinking, moral thinking, cultural thinking and social thinking. The writing of the judgment documents is a compulsory course and a regular course in the profession of the judges.

VIII. The art of interpreting the law

In judicial practice, the judge is a legal practitioner who utilizes the law mechanically, or creatively applies the law by the ways of interpreting the law and discovering the law, or create the applicable legal rules in the case of legal loopholes.

---

[16]Liu [14], p. 107.

Judges interpreting laws is a non-normative legal interpretation. Non-normative legal interpretation is mainly in the case of the legal provisions applicable to the case and the interpretation of legal facts, which in the traditional theoretical law is considered to be law application. The law application is mediated by legal interpretation.[17] The interpretation of the law is the professional technique and skill that the judge should have, and is the basic skill of the judge to handle cases. The legal provisions in the eyes of a judge are not rigid dogmas, and the judge must combine the living legal facts with the laws in the text to carry out multidimensional legal identification, legal judgment and legal interpretation. Throughout the process of adjudicating the case, we can find that there are not obvious connections between the legal spirit and legal significance of the legal provisions to be applied and the legal significance of the identified facts in many cases, especially in complex, difficult and new types of cases. It is required that the judge to question in legal sense, and to connect them with legal interpretation. The process of the judge's application of the law is in fact a re-creation process in which the judge understands the law, interprets the law, and reveals the legal spirit behind the legal provisions. Judges need to continue to cultivate and temper the skills of "finding law" and "making law" in this creative process. The basis of these skills is legal hermeneutics.

Judges must learn and study legal hermeneutics. For professional judges in judicial practice, legal interpretation is the jurisprudence of judge's occupation, the jurisprudence of judge's occupation skill, the most profound and original discipline foundation in occupation skill system of judges. Accordingly, the method of legal interpretation has become a profound and complex skill of judges' legal profession.

Why do we value the art connotation of judges' application and interpretation of the law? We are familiar with such a truth: in the rule of law society, the justice of the adjudication is ultimately measured by the rule of law principles. The implementation of the rule of law is reflected by the accuracy and scientificalness of the application of law, while the accuracy and scientificalness of the application of law depends on the proper and subtle legal interpretation. The slightest mistake of legal interpretation would inevitably lead to the improper application of law. This requires our judges to be faithfully loyal to the law, and be intelligently loyal to the law; not only to interpret the text in the legal dimension, but also reconstruct the legal spirit in the circumstance of legal incompetence; not only respect the judge's judgment based on individual reason and conscience, but also tolerantly understand and accept the legal awareness of natural justice from the legal community and even civil society.

Law application and the law interpretation in its process are by no means simple, mechanical installation and correspondence. We often have such experience, when the judge is applying laws, even if the bill at hand, he/she is often in confusion, the thinking process is often difficult, and even annoying and painful. Thus, in order to overcome the rashness, ambiguity and confusion of law interpretation, and to make the process of law interpretation into a comfortable and confident one, the judge must be lucrative, logical, experienced, and well grasping of mundane affairs; must moderately handle the case strictly by the bill, and keep pace with the times and

[17]Chen [15], p. 48.

pioneering and innovative; both to be courageous and good at breaking the theory and practice of dogma, but also abide by the stability of the law and predictability, be wary of caprice.[18] This occupation ethics shows the unique image and judge the mysterious status of the judge, but it is by no means artifacts, the high technology of the occupation distinguishes it from other occupations, making the group of judges a special professional group, requiring elitism. Judges' elite means that not all people are competent for judicial work. A competent judge must be a judge who is proficient in the legal interpretation of the law, that is to say, to be proficient in legal methods is the essential quality of the judge.[19] It is through the scientific interpretation of the law, the correct application of the law to express the concept of good and evil courage, thus becoming "outstanding character" legal person called by the German scholar Fred. This is the eternal pursuit of our professional judges to perfect ourselves.

The methods of legal interpretation include semantic interpretation, systematic interpretation, historical and teleological interpretation, restriction and expansion explanation, sociological interpretation. Judges use a variety of methods of legal interpretation to turn the law from the static, unconscious text into a dynamic, emotional expression tool, to make the law personality, to turn the trial into art.

XI. Judge legal promulgation art

The judicature is a profession emphasized on the negativity, thus the judge should always pay attention to their own words and deeds, be abide by the independence character, avoid making the parties and the civil society suspect that judges are biased, which would lead to the questioning on the process and results of the judicature. All of which seem to require the judge to stay away from the media, otherwise, not to say a lot of time and effort would put into it, frequently express themselves would inevitably be bound to have a slip of the tongue, and inadvertently expose their personal prejudice and superficialness to a large crowd; paying too much attention to the media is more vulnerable to the media control, and throwing the court into the community would throw the community into the court at the same time.[20] Therefore, in foreign countries, judges are not willing to communicate with the media, and moreover, many countries have set up a variety of institutional barriers to the media coverage of the judiciary. The quality of loneliness of judges in Western developed countries is quite obvious. The justices have high status and great influence, but they rarely appear in ordinary life, and there is no obligation to law propaganda for them, legal propaganda isn't the connotation of the judge's trail. However, in China, the judge must pay attention to the legal propaganda, which is the obligation of judges and one of the connotations of the judge's trial. Why are there so different propositions and conclusions? The reason is that the legal environment in the West is far from the legal background of China. Western countries have long advocated and praised the rule of law, the general quality of the people is generally high, the legal awareness of

[18] Kong [16], p. 7.
[19] Kong [17], p. 8.
[20] He [18], p. 267.

citizens is strong, the concept of the supremacy of law has been respected in society, as long as judging impartially, the judge has preached the law, interpreted the legal system. However, the reality of China's national quality and legal consciousness determines that our professional judges must use legal propaganda as an important part of professional skills to master and apply. This is also one important reason that why "The Organizational Law of the People's Court" takes legal propaganda as a judge's obligations. Meanwhile, I believe that our understanding of legal propaganda can not only stay at the level of the judge's obligation, but should rise to the level of the basic professional skills of judges. Although the particularity of the judges' profession requires the judges to keep a certain distance from the public and the mass media, the Chinese judges must have the techniques and skills of legal propaganda in the process of moving towards democracy and the rule of law. This is a pragmatism and empiricism Proposition—to establish a faith of the supremacy of law. On the one hand, the supremacy of the law requires judges to judge fairly according to law; on the other hand, the judges need to carry forward the spirit of law. On the one hand, the judge should pay attention to the professional characteristics of the judiciary, to maintain judicial independence; on the other hand, the judge should focus on the legal propaganda to optimize the effectiveness of the adjudication. A judge who is well versed in legal propaganda must pay more attention to the reality of the rule of law than to a judge who is not familiar with it, and pay more attention to the direction and the future of the rule of law. The judge trial better emphasize on the art infiltration of legal spirit, so that the legal resources are closer to the people's livelihood, and the behavior of citizens accept the rule of law gradually from passive to conscious.

X. Judge's execution art

In contrast to some foreign courts, our courts have the power to enforce the effective legal documents. The execution work is thus one of the important contents of the court's trial work, the execution of the adjudication order is the main content of the judge's trial. The execution work of the courts with Chinese characteristics also poses a high demand for judges' professional techniques and skills.

The execution power of the adjudication's command involves the jurisdiction and the administrative power, thus it is the cross-fusion of two powers with different nature, and has remarkable profession and skill. The difficulty in enforcement has not been effectively solved, partly because poor law enforcement environment and local protectionism is still serious, partly because the judge's art has not been substantially improved. The implementation of the referee order not only requires the judge to master the relevant legal knowledge, the implementation procedures, implementation ways and means, but also requires the judge to master the custom and culture, folk customs, legal culture, psychological knowledge, language skills, the behaving art and other comprehensive knowledge and skills. Only in this way, the judge can confidently deal with each case in a complex environment. The simple practice of "coercive" measures to "enforce" the implementation, the pursuit of quantity while ignoring the spiritual and emotional needs of the parties, even if it can not be said to be wrong, is also arbitrary and violent in many cases; not to mention a considerable part of the judge orders involving national coercive power to directly touch the field is neither simple nor easy. Therefore, judge's execution art does not require the judge to hold the batons, firearms, assault, but requires the judge to play the role of the facts-finder, commander and coordinator, emphasizes the method, concerns about effectiveness, comprehensively uses various means of implementation, tells the parties the importance of rights and interests, casts cultivation and influence, so that the law would maintain the true concern of human nature under the adjudication authority.

3 Sense of the Art of Adjudication

To raise the techniques and skills of the judge's trial to the level of art, is the design and creation of judges' professional skills in accordance with the laws of beauty and the value of happiness. The theoretical and practical significance of the judge's judicial art is, the judge occupation is designed to be the creator of the truth, the good and the beauty, judge's occupation techniques and skills can create greater welfare to the public, the spirit of law and the belief of the supremacy of law can be respected by the whole society, the function of judge occupation can play a greater role, the implementation of the law can truly realize people's happiness.

I. The art of adjudication and the overall quality of judges

The development of the judges' professional techniques and skills depends on the comprehensive promotion of the quality of judges, and taking the judges' professional skills as an artistic quality to train and advocate would surely promote the elite of the judges, which is a two-way interactive process.

1. Advocating the art of adjudication is helpful to improve the political quality of judges

Judicial trial belongs to the category of superstructure, and judicial power is an important part of the national public power, with strong characteristic of political, policy and moral, requiring the professional judges who exercise the judicial power to have excellent political quality. Judge's political quality is the basic content of the judge's overall quality constitution, which directly affects the trend of adjudication.

Judge only with the professional quality is not necessarily able to do a good job in the trial. Judge should also have a firm political stance, a clear political mind, a keen political vision and good political culture in the trial activity, and they must be good at forming the values of the judges' profession from the height of human nature, human conscience and social responsibility.

Judicial trial is closely linked to the historical period in which the magistrates are in their historical periods, with distinctive characteristics of the times. China's current professional construction of judges is moving forward in the direction needed by our new era, the background of the rule of law requires judges to practice political literacy, to purify and sublime the views on life and values that have been formed, to establish the correct system of adjudication value. A Chinese judge in modern sense should have excellent political quality, firmly establish the guiding ideology to carry out trial work around the overall situation, correctly understand and deal with the relationship between the judicial trial and the overall work of the party and the country, observing the situation from the political and overall situation, determine the focus of the trial work in different periods according to the needs of the times and the central government the deployment, put forward the corresponding trial measures and countermeasures for the actual situation; should be able to guide the practical activities with the important thought of the party, correctly handle the relationship between political theory and judicial practice, in the guidance of the party's line, principles, policies and the general goal of "three favorables", correctly apply the law and properly handle disputes. In the past, these requirements mainly rely on political education to carry out, but when it comes to now, only political study and preaching has been difficult to achieve, it is necessary to introduce new ways to cultivate the political and ideological qualities in the occupation education of judges. It is an effective way to carry out the humane education, the professional ethics education and the vocational skill artistic education of the legal profession by promoting the art of adjudication. The judge's judicial art is to maximize the pursuit of judicial justice under the guidance of the law of human nature, and to pursue justice from the perspective of human beauty.

Judicial justice is the eternal theme of judicial trial, is the basic requirement of the rule of law in the judicial work; without justice, judicial adjudication is worthless. In particular, at present, dealing with all kinds of complicated civil disputes in the period of social transformation, the judicial trial should not only to adhere to exercise judicial power independently in accordance with the law, but also to ensure fairness and justice in aspects of entity, procedure and image, only in this way can make the public and the litigants really recognize the social benefits brought by the judicial behavior, and make people feel good sense of justice.

With the development of China's market economy, the pluralism of economic subjects, the diversification of economic behavior and the independence of economic interests are more and more obvious, requiring professional judges to reach a certain political height in the trial work, pay attention to social development and the people's livelihood, give political cultivation with a new times connotation. The cultivation and training of judges' judicial art is a positive response to the needs of the times of political and ideological quality.

At the same time, standing in the final position of social contradictions and disputes, the judges should have the final consciousness of thorough solution to the dispute, which requires the judge to have a high degree of political sensitivity and perception, a strong sense of social responsibility and the overall situation, to comprehensively apply the trial art so as to actively and securely deal with group and multiple events and cases with greater social influence in special circumstances and sensitive times, in order to realize the unification of legal effect and seek the social effect and political effect.

2. Advocating the art of judge's trial helps to improve the professional ethics of judges

The quality of art originates in the quality of the creator.

If we define the adjudication as a professional art, then the judge's professional quality will directly determine the quality of the judicial trial, the judge's professional ethics determine the level and quality of judicial work to a large extent, so that abstracting the judge profession into a professional art will promote judges' professional ethics standards and professional ethics. The moral character not only represents the personal image of the judge, but also represents the professional spirit of the judiciary, and the progressive values and morality.[21] Only if the judges have perfect moral quality in themselves, they can correctly judge the good and evil by the socialist moral standards, the laws of beauty and the values of happiness, with the power of judges' morality to support the rule of law, to promote the concept of justice.

Judge's professional ethics refer to the sum of the ethical ideas and moral behaviors that judges follow in fulfilling their duties,[22] and they are the aesthetic support of the judge's trial art. All the judges' professional techniques and skills should be raised to the level of art, which is based on good morality. In a sense, professional ethics is the soul of judge's judicial art. Only on the basis of good professional ethics, the judge's judicial art will have professional characteristics and strong vitality. Judge's judicial art has put forward higher request to the occupation moral quality of judges, which requires judges to improve in six aspects, including guaranteeing judicial fairness, improving judicial efficiency, ensuring honest and upright, complying with judicial ceremonies, strengthening self-cultivation, restricting the activities outside the profession.[23] Strengthening the occupation moral cultivation of judges is helpful to establish the faith of the supremacy of law in judges' occupation, to develop a dedicated professional loyalty, prudent and rigorous work style, and integrity of the professional character, to reach a high degree of self-discipline. Only be faithful in law and firmly establish the concept of supremacy of law, judges can regard the legal profession as a professional art to practice, can have a more profound and understanding on the spirit, the essential role, the principle, the value standard and the application of law in accords with the needs of the times, can consciously exert the professional techniques and skills to illustrate the spirit of fairness, justice, democracy pursued by the law throughout the adjudication, can consciously standardize and guide the judges with the modern judicial ideas such as procedural justice, open and equality, honesty and efficiency. Only regard the judge occupation as a professional art, it is able to promote the occupation groups of judges to respect the rule of law in the handling process and make up for the defects of legal lag and loopholes, in the whole society, to establish a good professional image of professional judges, who are open minded, flexible, humane, respectful towards good, kindness and beautiful,

[21]Qiao [19], p. 6.

[22]Qiao [19], p. 6.

[23]See "*The Basic Rules on Professional Ethics of Judges of the People's Republic of China*", issued on October 18, 2001.

to make the adjudication be adapted to the needs of the time, so that become an important force in maintaining social order, promoting social progress and advancing the modernization of the rule of law; the judges are only loyal to their legal profession and regard their profession as an art and a career to pursue, would endeavor to pursue justice in order to achieve the happiness of the people, would be able to withstand mill and test, afford loneliness and poverty in the handling process, so as to defend the honor of judge profession with noble professional ethics. In addition, the judge's profession is very practical and operational, which requires the judges to have a prudent and rigorous work style, and the creation of art is built on prudence and rigor. Without a careful and rigorous work attitude and behavior, it is impossible for judges to cultivate the job into a career, and not to mention into an art; without the character of upright and outspoken, abhorrence of evil, believing in the supremacy of law, being unflinching to power, it is difficult for judges to keep calm and rational, and have courage to discard the false and retain the true, and uphold justice in the impetuous social environment.

3. Advocating the art of adjudication is helpful to improve the professional techniques and skills of judges

The empirical character of judicial occupation requires judges should have superb occupation techniques and skills, which require long-term training through judicial practice, in which the training methods include undergraduate, master and doctoral degree education before judicial practice, and judicial practice education and training during practice. The continuity of learning and comprehension process study give judges the opportunity the provisions of the laws, and help judges to understand the source, the jurisprudence and the spirit of the law, the continuous accumulation process is the process of judge's skills gradually from mechanical operation to the artistic.

There is no ultimate mode of judge's judicial art, and there is no end of our pursuit of art. The ideal to artistic has prompted the judge to constantly expand the horizon of legal theory research, to introduce new legal theory and research dynamic into the visual field, to improve the logical thinking ability, the perceived ability, the quick response and coping ability, written expression ability. At the same time, the traits of art never limit the skills of the judicial trial to the field of jurisprudence, but to the fields of philosophy, politics, economics, logic, sociology, management, media, aesthetics, psychology, art, literature and other disciplines, learn from the various methods that can be used. Therefore, the judge who pursues the art of trial must pay attention to broaden the scope of knowledge in order to accumulate rich connotation and heritage. Only those who insist on hard work in judicial practice, and constantly improve the literature, music, art, sculpture, painting and other elegant art appreciation ability, explore elegant hobbies, cultivate noble sentiments and refined temperament, and integrate other social sciences with legal science, can raise the judicial professional techniques and skills to the artistic level.

II. The art of judge's trial and judicial capacity

Strengthening the construction of judicial capacity is not only the requirement of strengthening the party's ruling ability, but also the inherent requirement of the judicial profession, and the requirement of the judge's occupation of the times. Judicial capacity includes the ability to control the court, the ability to mediate, the ability to write judgment documents and the ability to apply the law. In these "four abilities", the ability to apply the law is in the core position, the ability to control the court is the precondition of applying the law, litigation mediation ability is the best legal means to build a harmonious society, and writing judgment documents ability is comprehensive reflection of the ability to control the court and the ability to apply the law. These four abilities are the basic skills of professional judges, and the components of the professional construction of judges. To emphasize the judge's judicial art is to take these four abilities as an important part of the training of the judges' professional skills.

1. Advocating the art of judge's judicial trial is helpful to improve the ability to control the court

In the modern sense, the judicial trial has put forward high demand to the court hearing, and the reform of the trial mode has been carried out with the court hearing as the core for years. The new trial idea and trial mode require judges to give full play to the function and role of the court hearing, regarding the courtroom as a public confrontation where the rights and obligations of the parties confront, meanwhile, as a stage where the judge exhibits the judicial skills, talent and occupation charming. Whether the court hearing function is fully realized lies in whether the judge can successfully control the court. If the judges can master the art of controlling the court, they would provide an open negotiation, dialogue, and debate opportunity for the parties, thus to realize social justice in a way that can been seen by the parties and the public.

The court hearing has the functions of ensuring the fairness of the procedure, the fairness of the entity, the fairness of the form and the justice of the judge's image, guiding the public to abide by the law, educating the public to standardize their own words and deeds, embodying the social mainstream values, and maintaining the orderly development of society.[24] Still, the court hearing has the function of enhancing the economic efficiency. Modern court hearing has carried out the principles of direct speech, the principle of procedural autonomy, and the principle of punctual procedure. In judicial practice, it is implemented that the technical rules of the application rate of verdict and simple procedure, which greatly improves the efficiency of trial and helps reducing the human, material and financial resources in the trial process, optimizing the allocation of judicial resources, and maximizing the judicial efficiency.[25]

---

[24]Qiao [20], pp. 19–20.

[25]Qiao [21], p. 20.

The art of court hearing is the rationality, the scientificity and the practicability of the method and the way of controlling and directing litigation as shown by the judge in the process of hearing the case. The reason why the court controlling should be metaphor as an art, is that the judge on the court shows not only the judge's trial skills, but also the judge's long-term academic accomplishment and cultural heritage. Once the connotation of culture be sublimated would turn into art, and art has never been separated with culture. Written art emphasizes "effort out of writing", poetry art emphasizes "effort out of poetry", the art of court hearing emphasizes "effort out of courtroom". If a judge wants to hold a good court hearing, not just he/she remembers a few legal provisions and legal knowledge, but rather has got an accumulation of long-term judicial experience and natural integration with cultural accomplishment. The artistic beauty of a successful court hearing and the beauty of the other forms of art are essentially the same or similar in nature, and there are many similarities between the forms and methods of the expression. The art of controlling the court emphasizes the judge in the trial to accurately control the time, the line, the atmosphere and the pace of the trial stages, so that the whole trial process would be simple and neat, natural and smooth, focused on important disputes, and litigants would have the opportunity to argue in the court hearing. In such a small courtroom, it is able to debate no matter win or lose, how unlimited the art space is!

2. Advocating the art of judge's judicial trial helps to improve the ability of mediation

In the Confucian culture tradition as the main line of the Chinese realistic society, building a harmonious society has always been our ideal. Mediation is an effective means to build a harmonious society, and thus has been one of the important ways to resolve disputes in our society. Whether it is official mediation or civil mediation, or mediation hold by guild organization, are flashing a harmonious light of wisdom. Litigation mediation is the most important form of official mediation, and it is an important way for people's court to deal with disputes in realistic context. It is the necessary constitution of the art of judge's trail. Litigation mediation fully embodies the beauty of harmony and order. Order is the form of harmony, harmony is always built on the order; the beauty represents the real harmony, harmony is the expression of beauty, and "is the harmony and unity between man and nature, subject and object, reason and sensibility, freedom and necessity, the purpose of practice and the law of the objective world."[26] It is harmony and order that constitutes the intersection of law and beauty;[27] and it is harmony and order that forms the aesthetic value of litigation mediation.

The art of litigation mediation encourages judges to do meticulous ideological work of both parties in the process, through legal interpretation and education to help them improve their awareness and consciousness, strengthen the concept of law, prompting them to resolve the dispute through dialogue and consultation calmly. At

[26]Lv [22], p. 430. Quoted in Laixiang [23], p. 73.
[27]Lv [22], p. 430. Quoted in Laixiang [24], p. 432.

the same time, the art of litigation mediation also encourages judges to improve the efficiency of handling cases, reduce the cost of litigation, and save judicial resources.

3. Advocating the art of judge's judicial trial is helpful to improve the judge's writing ability

The writing of judgment documents is an important part of the trial work of the court, and it is also a regular work for the judge to perform the duty of trial assigned by the Constitution and the law. With the gradual deepening of the judicial reform, especially the reform of the trial mode, people's understanding of the importance of the judgment documents is deepening day by day. The judgment document is not only the written notice of the court to announce the verdict of the adjudication, but also an important carrier to show the judicial ideas of litigation democracy, procedural disclosure and judicial justice in the modern society.

As we all know, open trial is an important judicial principle in modern society rule of law. The process of public adjudication plays an important role in preventing judicial arbitrariness, curbing judicial corruption and realizing judicial justice. Judicial openness is not only the openness of the court hearing, but also the openness of judgments and verdicts. Where there is transparency, where there is justice. The functions of the modern judicial documents, including the function of the result notice, the function of recording the procedure, the function of the judgment reasoning, the function of the behavioral paradigm and the function of judicial management,[28] are all need to be realized by judges' careful creations.

At present, the biggest problem in the writing of the judgment documents is the weakness in reasoning, thus the function of the judgment reasoning, the function of the behavioral paradigm can not be reflected through the judgment documents. In the case that the judgment doesn't explain the reasons for the judgment, the public would not be able to understand the judge basis of the judge's decision; do not open the process of judge's free evaluation of the evidence, the public would not understand the path of the judge's thought; the referee does not explain the judgment reason, it is very likely to conceal some favoritism or corrupt behavior, and leave an opportunity for judicial corruption. Therefore, the written of judgments and verdicts reflects not only the judges' writing capacities, but also the speculative ability, as well as the ability towards justice, and it has to do with the image of the judges, the image of the courts, and the image of the judiciary of China.

China's ancient "judges"[29] pioneers, such as Bai Juyi, Su Shi, all have a set of comprehensive quality and heritage of literary experts, jurists, politicians and artists. They use the superb judgment writing skills to write so far well-known graceful judgments, which are the judge's judicial art reflected in the referee writing. Advocating the judge's judicial art, is to encourage judges to create the judgments documents as artwork, to write the judgment documents with profound legal literacy cultural

[28]Qiao [25], pp. 137–138.

[29]In acient China, the occupation judge hasn't been classified separately, but served by official who exercised the administrative and judicial functions simultaneously.

knowledge, to write a wonderful judgment with the wisdom and originality of a profession judge!

4. Advocating the art of judge's judicial trial is helpful to improve the ability of applying law

Judges resolve disputes with the application of law as a bridge.

The application of the law means the specialized work that the judge, with his/her own legal knowledge and judicial professional skills, applies the law properly and accurately to the specific case, and draws the conclusion of the judgment, so as to effectively eliminate the dispute. Correctly applying the law is the basic requirements of the judges' profession, and also the basic guarantee of judging for judges. The application of law is a kind of subjective thinking process which uses logic and empirical way of thinking to understand, judge and choose the law. This kind of thinking method requires long-term legal practice to achieve the level of sophistication. In addition to profound legal knowledge, it also requires long-term judicial practices and summarized experiences. The profession of judges is the profession of experiences, and the trick of applying the law lies in the summary and application of experiences. Without the skills training of the legal application, the judging level can not be really improved. The application of the law is the finishing touch of the judge's professional skills. The judges can not be satisfied with the role of "vending machine" of the law, just relying on logical rules to draw the conclusion of the judgments, and should fully grasp the various methods of applying laws, give full play to their intelligence and creativity in the process of applying laws.

In the case of a trial, a judge must interpret and explain the legal provisions to be applied, that is, the exercise of judicial interpretation. The power of judicial interpretation in the common law countries has a quasi-legislative status, thus the British judge can make law in its unique open legal system, or even "judge without law"[30] on individual cases, not only apply the law, but also make the law. China belongs to the continental legal system in law application, although cannot perform judge-made law in accordance with the rules of the common law, but because the static nature of the legal rules, in order to achieve the legal goals set, it cannot do without the creative interpretation and application. Therefore, our judges can apply the law creatively through the method of legal interpretation. The necessity for the judges' power to explain the law and the gradual expansion of the scope of interpretation provides a broader space for the art of adjudication.

The professionalization of judges is not only to identify the judge occupation as a simple occupation, but shape the judge's professional groups into elite groups in a deeper background and level. To master the methods and skills of legal application is an important way to realize the superiorization of the judge group. Meanwhile, emphasizing the correct application of the law in the judicial practice, and taking the ability of law application as the focus of the art of adjudication, are not only to ensure the correct interpretation, application of the law, and the fair judgments, but

[30]Chen [26]. p. 69.

also hope to promote the professionization construction of judges by enhancing the ability of the application of law, in order to gain public recognition and respect for the judge's professional groups, to maintain the enduring charm of the occupation.

4 Characteristics of Judges' Judicial Art

Based on the special nature of the judge's profession and the unique law of judicial action, judicial art has its own professional attributes, such as legality, programmatic, empirical, complexity, creativity, culture, sociality, artistic, technicality, ideology, and so on.

I. Legal characteristics

The judge exercises the judicial power given by the Constitution and the law, and the source of judicial power is the law, the basis of the adjudication is also the law. The legality is the most fundamental feature of the art of adjudication. First of all, the judge must establish the faith of the supremacy of law, only subject to the law and legal spirit, take the legal belief as the most basic professional ethics and quality, and should not succumb to secular and power. Secondly, the judge must correctly understand the intent of the law, interpret the substantive content of the legal provisions in accordance with the spirit of the law and the purpose of legislation, no misinterpretation, no misunderstanding, not misuse, and correctly understand the boundaries among law, morality and policy. Finally, the judge must exercise the judicial power within the limits prescribed by law, promote lawsuit in accordance with the legal procedures, and must not exceed the boundaries delineated by the law to achieve the effect of pseudo art by unlawful means. The legality is the precepts that judges must follow. Judges should not only accept the legal constraints, but also use legal weapons to punish and put an end to all illegal acts in litigation activities, so that the litigation activities can run on the track of the legal system. In order to match to the legality of the art of adjudication, the judge must pay attention to the renewal of new information and legal knowledge of the legislation. For the latest legislation of the legislature and the latest judicial interpretation of the Supreme People's Court and the Supreme People's Procuratorate, the judge should grasp and understand in a timely manner to ensure the correctness of the application of law and the unity of the legal system.

II. Procedural characteristics

Procedural justice and substantive justice constitute the concept of justice.

In addition to substantive justice, judicial justice includes procedural justice. Without the guarantee of legal procedure, it is very difficult for the judicial process to guarantee the legitimacy of the substantive conclusion. The judge's judicial art is the art which is established on the due process, and the art will deviate from the right direction without the due process.

To solve any problem, there must be some ways, and there must be a scientific process, that is procedure. Judges must follow the procedures prescribed by law, and the expansion space of professional art should be based on strict procedural norms. According to the procedural characteristics of the stage, the judge operates the adjudication strategy, and seeks the possible variables of the substantive law in the constant dimension of the procedural law, so as to realize the justice of the adjudication.

Why should judges follow the idea of procedural justice? Procedural justice is an experience of the practice of the rule of law in China and foreign countries. The procedure for the case is first a dispute resolution mechanism equal in the form and the pattern, so the dispute resolution mechanism must have a predetermined form and pattern, or else the foundation of the construction of the dispute resolution mechanism would disappear. Different procedures would naturally have different trial results, and not all procedures can lead to fair results. It is not surprising that some Westerners say "procedure determines fairness".[31]

Western procedural justice can be interpreted through the famous O. J. Simpson murder case in the United States, although the conclusion of this case is difficult to accept for many people. From the procedure of the Simpson case, both the United States and the Chinese public were convinced that Simpson was the murderer of his ex-wife and ex-wife's boyfriend, Simpson absolutely constituted intentional homicide. However, due to the flaws in the evidence collection process, the evidence could not be used as evidence, although the evidence could directly prove the defendant's crime. The American public accepted the seemingly bizarre judgment made by the judge because the people generally agreed that Simpson had received a fair trial of the statutory procedures, and that the judge's refusing to accept the evidence obtained by the police because of the discriminatory reason was consistent with the requirements of the procedural justice. According to the procedural law of the United States, it was the only conclusion of the court that Simpson was innocence. However, if the case occurred in China, Simpson would have no chance to escape the legal sanction, the people would strongly urged to punish the culprits through a variety of ways, the judicial organs would have to carefully consider the people's wrath, and choose substantive justice rather than procedural justice.

The purpose and value of the principle of procedural justice is to sacrifice the individual's justice and interests in exchange for the overall justice and interests. In a society that advocates procedural justice, people choose to protect the majority justice and interests, even in some cases where the state indulges the criminals to escape the punishment of the law, but maintains the unity and fairness of the procedure so that everyone can be treated in the same or similar way and avoid being tortured, so as to prevent injustice. In 2005, the media-hype She Xianglin murder case was a bitter fruit of lack of procedural justice. Envisage in the investigation and prosecution stage, if there had been no torture, if there had been no extorting confessions by torture, if there had been no strong pressure from the families of the victims and the so-called

[31] Liu [27], p. 100.

coordination from politics and law committee and the interferes from other external factors, if the court had adhered to strict procedures rules, would the injustice occur? Therefore, the sacrifice of the justice of the legal procedure would lead to more injustice of the adjudication. So, we believe that procedural justice is the inherent content of the art of adjudication.

III. Empirical characteristics

> The idea of the pursuit of the law is closely related to the life experience of law, and the experience of the cultural and historical environment of a particular society is helpful for people to understand the goal of law itself. Law is a summary of the experience of the people in a particular culture. Life experience has an important influence on the idea of law.
>
> —Han Dayuan, The history and idea of East Asia's rule of law.

Legal science always goes hand in hand with experience, and the development of law comes from the abstraction and reflection of experience rather than the fantasy of general logic. The trial experience of judges is the original material and basis of the trial art. It is difficult to form a superb trial art without the practical experience of the judge.

Experience refers to the perceptual knowledge in practice. Judge trial experience is the accumulation and summary of a variety of emotional knowledge in the trial practice. Perceptual knowledge begins with the practice feeling, and when this feeling accumulates to a certain extent, there would be regularity, empirical, and be accepted by judges, and the positive and the effective rules and the experience become the source of the trial art.

In judicial practice, judges tend to rely on experience to determine the facts of the case, find the corresponding laws, there is much more experience, experience strongly affects the subjective tendency of the judge in the judgment process, with inspiration and enlightenment. In the judicial occupation career, the judge will more or less accumulate experiences, some of which with similarities, some of which with individual character, but all originating in the judge's first case and becoming increasingly rich with the extension of career. It is difficult to obtain the empirical judicial experience through the reading theory monograph, and the judge must make it more mature through the professional training and daily self-improvement.

Judge's experience has the characteristics of intuitive, practical, dynamic, diversity, creative, and professional. The judge as an ordinary person, in the process of the adjudication, he/she will have intuition and stubbornly influence thinking, which is a basic form of experience. "Five Observing", the way China's ancient "judges" took when hearing cases, is a fixed rule of intuitive experience. The practicality of the experience is the recurrence and specificity of experience, more practice, more opportunities for experience to be tested, more opportunities for experience to be corrected, and richer the content and the level of experience. At the same time, the accumulation of experience is a dynamic and diversified process, which is based on the different characteristics of the judge's case and the continuous development of the judge's personal ability of the case, and the experience accumulated by the different judges would present a variety of tendencies because of the differences in the personality of the judge. The dynamics and diversity of experience also reflects the creativity of the judges in the process of empirical formation. The experiences of the judge may be partly derived from the results of the predecessors, but most of them come from the observation and reflection of the specific cases of the judge individual, and the specific of the case and the unavoidable subjectivity of the judge's decision together determine the creativity of the judge's experience and become a professional feature.

From the perspective of philosophical epistemology, the judge's trial is constrained by the rule of thumb on the basis of intuitive knowledge. No matter how high the judge's judicial art is, it can not be divorced from the profound influence of experience, on the contrary it is the reflection of mature experience. Although we have no intention of equating the judge's judgment with the experience of the judge's trial and no intention of lifting a simple empiricism; we can not deny the connection between the art of adjudication and the experience of the judge's trial: the inspiration of art comes from the inspiration of experience, the creativity of art comes from the richness of experience, the persistence of art comes from the changes of the experience, the beauty of art comes from the polish of experience, and the maturity of art comes from the sublimation of experience.

IV. Complexity characteristics

The complexity of the art of adjudication is embodied in the following aspects: First, the combination of knowledge, that is, the art of adjudication is the result of the use of multidisciplinary knowledge by judges, involving philosophy, law, ethics, sociology, economics, psychology, literature, aesthetics, logic, communication, public relations, and so on. The judge should be an inter-disciplinary talent, should also have the knowledge system of social science and the knowledge base of natural science, and be able to explore the positive solution of social problems by comparing with the truth criterion of natural science. Secondly, the composite of experience, that is, the art of adjudication is about the dual role of the experience of judges' judicial practice and social life experience. The experience of the adjudication comes from the whole process of the case, with significant judicial characteristics, the traces of the rule of law are clearly discernible, the legal community often has the same adjudication experience; social experience from the judge's personal social life, including personal experience, close distant facts or even long distant events, with uncertainty, non-normative, obvious personality characteristics, strong randomicity, difficult to follow its laws. The commonality of judges' trial experience and the diversity of social experience determines that the art of adjudication has a lawful and creative space, which is a balance between commonality and individuality, and a true imagination based on established model.

V. Creative characteristics

Repetition makes people tired and creativity yearning. The art of life lies in the creation, and the creativity is the foundation of the development of art. Without creation, art would no longer exist.

Under the rule of law, the judge is a silent person, a conservative person. But the judge is also a thoughtful person, a wise person, whose initiative upon the law can make the judge consciously break through old ideas, creatively apply the law, creatively use the legal principles, and achieve the value of the rule of law. The judges who understand the rule of law from the value level get rid of the shackles of handling the cases mechanically, and lay the foundation for the art of adjudication. The standard of handling the case mechanically does not include the judge's creativity, but even exclude it; while the standard of handling the case artistically protects and encourages the judge to consider the justice standards and the justice ways of the law application according to the changes of the world and the law, thus fix the stationary legal provisions with the changeable social life closely, and activate the adaptability of law to reality.

The judge's creativity advocated by the art of adjudication doesn't mean requesting the judge to pursue a simple arbitrary non-repetition, but to ask the judge to rationally and correctly perform the adjudication function on the complex knowledge system and experience system, to realize the harmony and beauty of art. The judicial methods, those simply pursuing of novelty, personality, ignoring the unity of the legal system and deviating from the spirit of law, are not artistic, and also contrary to the basic rules of adjudication, not worth advocating.

VI. Cultural characteristics

Educated person (cultural being) has always been salvation enthusiasm. Judge is considered an educated person.

The cultural characteristics of judge profession have a profound impact on the art of adjudication: the strength of the cultural characteristics depends on the cultural concept of the judge, and the judge's cultural concept determines the value orientation and content of the art. The judge's positive culture idea will lead the judge to listen to the voice of the people, support the poor and the weak, and make art full of vigour because of its relevance to civil society. On the contrary, if there is no rich cultural connotation to support, the adjudication would be mechanical, boring, lack of intellectual.

The adjudications of any age are deeply imprinted on the culture of contemporary culture, with different cultural characteristics. Professional judges live in the cultural atmosphere of the times, the process of the growth of judges is also the process of cultural infiltration, the concept of professional art and behavior can not be separated from the cultivation of specific culture, especially the legal culture. The experience of traditional and realistic civilization, and the cognition, overcoming, absorbing and drawing lessons of Chinese and foreign cultures, lay the foundation for the formation of judges' style. Different cultural heritage would form a different adjudication style, and we could easily identify the cultural connotation and artistic composition of the adjudication from the judgment documents, the last carrier of the adjudication.

VII. Social characteristics

Law lies in the society, and judges are also normal people, without the social life and practice, the law and the judges are meaningless. The occupation is there to solve the imbalance of social relations, to seek legal relationship that has already been hurt to heal, make social life back to the track set by law, to make the social members enjoy peace and convenience brought by the rule of law. The adjudication method violating the social demand, as well as authoritarian law that ignores the social psychological endurance, is easy to impair the life of the rule of law, not to mention the beauty of art. Therefore, the judge must pay attention to the national economy and the people's livelihood, consider the social psychology, realize the social awareness, and serve the social life. The art of adjudication has obvious sociological characteristics.

The judge's knowledge and experience comes from the practice of social life, the value of the judge's professional skills can only be realized in the process of serving the society. Society is a "University", to complete the academic education would lay a good foundation for the legal profession, and more knowledge needs to be learned in social practice. All the really important legal questions come from social life, originated in the intensifying social contradictions, some are sharp, some are gentle, but it is the result of the distribution anomie of social interests, which requires the exploring of the coordination path from sociological perspective, the supplying the blank of legal experience with social experience. The legal person completely cultivated by colleges can only solve the problem of books, can not correspond the diversity of social life with the rigid theoretical principle, can not deeply understand the origin of the problem, the crux of the problem, the depth of the problem and the multi dimension of the problem. Different social life levels reflect the different characteristics of the problem, for example, the judge dealing with marriage and family cases, if there is a marriage experience, he/she would be able to better understand the social characteristics of marriage and family problems, so as to conform to social conscience and feelings, to judge fairly. Therefore, the accumulation of social experience provides a vivid material for the legal person's thinking, so that the legal person's judgment process is close to the people's life experience, has the common sense, reflects the judicial democracy.

At the same time, social identity is one of the important criteria for examining the artistic nature of the adjudicature and the scientific nature of justice. The law application is the duty of the judge, but it is not a linear, rigid process, and the judge has a certain discretion in the process of applying the law. Different judges may apply different laws in dealing with same kind of problems, and even if the same law is applied, different interpretations may be made. Even if the results of the interpretation are the same, the decisions of the entity are still likely different. Therefore, the evaluation of the judge's trial can not only take applying to the law as the standard, the results of the adjudications also need to be tested by society. In the context of the current concern about the stability of social order and the emphasis on the beauty of social harmony, judges should constantly explore the social function and social effect of the adjudication and seek the connection between the rule of law and social identity.

Therefore, the art of adjudication can not be separated from social practice, the adjudication can not be separated from the recognition of the community, and the effectiveness of the adjudication can not be separated from the examination of society. Society is the training of the school of the judges' art, is the drill field and exhibit hall of the art of adjudication. Only by deeply integrating into the social life, the art of adjudication can have vitality and development prospects.

VIII. Artistic characteristics

The law has artistic value, and the judges' profession has artistic value as well. The legal system itself is a "practical art".[32] The act of the judge is the bright between "law as art" to "art of law", "law as art" and the conclusion of "law is art" is only one step away. As an explanatory model, the most important significance of "law as art" is that the transformation of the legal theory from "scientific" to "artistic" has begun, and legal philosophy begins to be based on the ontology of art and the doctrine of law has to rethink in the light of the legal art.[33]

The judicial process is a rational process, one can and should use language to tell; at the same time, the judicial process is a process beyond reason, is a mysterious, unspeakable process, both scientific and artistic process, so that the judicial practice becomes art.[34] Throughout the whole process of the judicial practice, art also lies in the connotation of the judge's judicial art. As the characteristics of perceptual knowledge, art embodies the concern for human nature and the respect of human rights in the process and the conclusion of the adjudication, revealing the justice of the judiciary itself and the judge's personality charm.

IX Technical characteristics

The art of adjudication is a kind of abstract and macroscopic feeling, but it can also be measured and expressed by the quantitative and intuitive index, and the specific index is the technical content of the adjudication.

Judge's judicial art is the sublimation of professional techniques and skills, based on the rich technical characteristics. First of all, professional techniques and skills are of fundamental significance in the art of adjudication. In addition to the background of the college education, judges should also be trained in legal profession. Our university education is not generally offered courses of legal methods, judges have rare opportunity to study legal skills before inauguration, so they have to make up the classes after inauguration; even the makeup, it is not systematic and standardized. If there is no hard practice, such a professional basis is difficult to reach the art of adjudication. Therefore, the cultivation of legal profession is the only way for the judge changing from the case-handling machine to the freedom of art. Secondly,

[32] Lv [28], p. 150.
[33] Lv [29], p. 550.
[34] Lv [30], pp. 555–556.

as far as the adjudication, the professional techniques and skills have the progressive characteristics. The training of vocational skills is not a day of work, and it requires continuous learning, practicing, and accumulating. The best way to cultivate a professional skill is to practice, and the best teacher is the judge himself/herself. The process of the adjudication turning to art is also the process of gradual accumulation, refining professional techniques and skills for judges, and it is endless. The basic and progressive nature of the judges' professional techniques and skills determines that the technical characteristics of the judge's trial cover the whole process of the professionalism of the judges.

X Ideological characteristics

The most precious wealth of human beings is thought.

The centerpiece of the judge's judicial art is the judge's thought. The judge's judicial art is a collection of professional judges, a treasure trove of thought. Without thoughts, a judge has no soul, let alone art. Ideology is an important feature of the judge's judicial art.

Judge's trial is a process of the generation of old thought and new thought, and it is a process of speculation, a process of continuous reflection of thoughts. The ideology of the judge's judicial art is embodied in two aspects: first, the judges who know the art of adjudication are the professionals good at thinking, diligent in thinking, brave in thinking, and accustomed to constantly reflect on the meaning of law, the value of the law and the legal method that should be reformed in order to realize the rule of law in the process of the adjudication. Secondly, the judges who know the art of adjudication are the professionals who can express their thoughts and legal accomplishment in the process of adjudication, full of sense of responsibility to the society, from the procedure details to the final conclusion of the adjudication, there are mature legal thoughts and dialectical philosophy thoughts of the judges.

References

1. Li S (2001) Introduction to art. Communication University of China Press, pp 6–72
2. Chen W (2004) The development of China artistic image: on the relationship between the development of aesthetic consciousness and artistic image in China. Xuelin Press, pp 1–2
3. Ueda B (2004) Twelve lectures on modern art (trans: Feng Z). Hunan Literature and Art Publishing House, p 47
4. Taine HA (2004) Philosophy of art (trans: Fu L). Tianjin Social Press, pp 34–62
5. Hendrik Willem VL (1938) The arts of mankind. George G. Harrap & Co. LTD, p 23
6. Cardozo BN (1931) Mr. Justice Holmes. Harv Law Rev, 44(5):682–692
7. Cardozo BN (1931) Mr. Justice Holmes. Harv Law Rev, 44(5):682–684
8. Lv S (2004) The truth, goodness and beauty of law: primary exploration of legal aesthetics. Law Press China, p 555
9. Cardozo BN (1931) Mr. Justice Holmes. Harv Law Rev, 44(5):683
10. Gadamer H-G (1975) Truth and method (trans: Weinsheimer J, Marshall DJ). Continuum Publishing Group, p 84

11. Huang J (2004) Informal discussion on the art of court hearing, People's Evening, B2. May 17th
12. Liu J (2003) Enjoy the law: a legal professional's thought note. Law Press·China, p 105
13. Liu J (2003) Enjoy the law: a legal professional's thought note. Law Press·China, p 106
14. Liu J (2003) Enjoy the law: a legal professional's thought note. Law Press·China, p 107
15. Chen J (1999) The philosophy of the law interpretation. Shandong People's Publishing House, p 48
16. Kong X (2004) The method of legal interpretation and case study. People's Court Press, p 7
17. Kong X (2004) The method of legal interpretation and case study. People's Court Press, p 8
18. He W (1998) The idea and system of the judicature. China University of Political Science and Law Press, p 267
19. Qiao X (2003) Judges literacy and ability training. Law Press·China, p 6
20. Qiao X (2003) Judges literacy and ability training. Law Press·China, p 19–20
21. Qiao X (2003) Judges literacy and ability training. Law Press·China, p 20
22. Lv S (2004) The truth, goodness and beauty of law: primary exploration of legal aesthetics. Law Press·China, p 430
23. Laixiang Z (2007) Beauty is harmony. Shandong University Press, p 73
24. Laixiang Z (2007) Beauty is harmony. Shandong University Press, p 432
25. Qiao X (2003) Judges literacy and ability training. Law Press·China, pp 137–138
26. Chen J (1999) The philosophy on legal interpretation. Shandong People's Publishing House, p 69
27. Liu X (2003) West window & law rain. Law Press·China, p 100
28. Lv S (1997) Study on contemporary western jurisprudence. China Renmin University Press, p 150
29. Lv S (2004) The truth, goodness and beauty of law: primary exploration of legal aesthetics. Law Press·China, p 550
30. Lv S(2004) The truth, goodness and beauty of law: primary exploration of legal aesthetics. Law Press·China, pp 550–556

Chapter 2
The Theoretical Foundation of the Art of Adjudication

Law is the intersection point of ideal and reality. Like a lotus, its roots penetrate the soil, but the buds and flowers stretch into the sky. The law is an art that transforms the friction of material interests into the ideal value of light.
—Wu Jingxiong, The Art of Law

The art of adjudication is to liberate the personality of the judicial officer, so that the judicial officer can show the individual charms of the judgment and value persuits.[1] The personality of the judge's trail is not the temperament, character and habits of the individual, but the extension of the character and style of the law based on the theory of jurisprudence. Therefore, the aesthetic beauty of the trial art has the common characteristics of the legal theory, and the vitality of the trial art is its deep legal connotation and spiritual essence. The adjudication art only roots in jurisprudence and related disciplines such as the philosophy of law and sociology of law to contend in beauty and fascination.

1 An Explanation of Law, Spirit of Law and the Art of Adjudication

The judge is handling the case according to law, then what is the law? What is the spirit of the law? What kind of legal spirit is the art of adjudication based on? As early as 2300 years ago in Athens, a brave little girl Antigone asks the eternal question on the word "law", "law, what is it?" The legend of Antigone has a brother who died in the war against the King. King Cleo issued a decree: the rebels were killed, and the corpses were abandoned under the city wall, nobody was allowed to mourn or bury the bodies, let the crow peck the beast. Anyone who violated this order would be stoned to death. The brave Antigone chose not to listen to this command, pushed away from the barrier of the guards, under the watchful eyes of the people, and buried her brother according to the old habits of worship. The soldiers dissatisfied with the "inhuman evil law" of the king, so no one "stone her to death" of the "law", just

[1] Tiechuan [1].

Y. Kai, *The Art of Trial Process*,
https://doi.org/10.1007/978-981-15-6434-5_2

arrested and brought Antigone before the king. "Do you know that you have broken the law?" Cleo, the king, growled and asked angrily. Antigone retorted sarcastically, "It was not Zeus who made that proclamation to me; nor was it Justice, who resides in the same house with the gods below the earth, who put in place for men such laws as yours. Nor did I think your proclamation so strong that you, a mortal, could overrule the laws of the gods, that are unwritten and unfailing."[2] What is the law? The answer to this simple question, human beings have been searching for thousands of years. Brave Antigone gives a surprisingly simple answer: the law is nature's justice and human feelings! Although Antigone was finally killed, but the natural law philosophy and theory of "within the law, there should be nature's justice and human feelings" spread in the world since then, giving birth to the principle of "the supremacy of law".[3] Throughout the ages, there are lots of the human understanding and answers for the question of what the law is, and so many questions on the legal spirit, so far there is no standard answer. I believe that the laws are the rules and regulations, which bring human rights, interests, peace, freedom, harmony, order, dignity, civilization and such kind of happiness, are the embodiment of human rationality, the social norms filled with poetic beauty and harmonious beauty, and the expression system of the truth, goodness and beauty of human nature. This is a personal understanding and interpretation of the nature of law, and it is an ideal description of law to abandon the inhuman and anti-human nature of evil law.

To jurists, the nature of law is not only a realistic expectation, but also a kind of eternal pursuit. The judge should have a more profound knowledge and understanding of the essence of law, for the value of law, the pursuit should be more concerned of human beauty. In the work "law", Plato said lawmakers should take into account all the virtues of the law. Virtue is divided into two categories: human and divine. The first virtue of human is health, the second is beauty, the third is strength, and the fourth is richness. The first virtue of divine is wisdom, the second is temperance, and the combination of the two gives birth to justice, and finally is bravery. When it comes to the law, Plato believed that everyone has two intentions in mind, one is the hope of happiness, and the second is the fear of suffering. People can think about the good and evil, such as hope, happiness, pain, and so on, and the thinking reflects in the state's decree called law.[4] Law, being essentially a restraint upon the exercise of arbitrary power, is hostile to anarchy as well as to despotism. It seeks to introduce order and regularity into the dealings of private individuals as well as the operations of governmental organs.[5] Therefore, although the law, including the boring, daunting coercion and intervention force, people are still uneasy to start the benign operation of legal power. This ambivalence is reflected in legislation, reflected in the law enforcement, and more reflected throughout the judiciary, which requires frequently reflection on the legal meaning of law, the virtue of law and the spirit of law when face the legal reality. For judges, to understand the laws, the legal norms

[2]Sophocles [2].

[3]Dingyu [3].

[4]He [4].

[5]Bodenheimer [5].

and the spirit of the laws, to interpret the morality of law by the judicial art, to overcome the tyranny of law, is a kind of aesthetic, with a rational behavior and way of thinking.

When talking about the relationship between aesthetics and hermeneutics, Gadamer pointed out, "If the task of hermeneutics is to be defined as the bridge between the individual and the historical distance between the two spirits, artistic expression seems to lie entirely outside the domain of hermeneutics. Of all the things that confront us in nature and history, it is the work of art that speaks most directly to us. It has a mysterious affinity, which holds our whole existence, seemingly without any distance, as if its daily encounter is with our own encounter."[6] He referred to Hagel's view of art as forms of Absolute Spirit, "he saw in art a form of Spirit's self-knowledge in which nothing alien and unredeemable appeared, a form in which there was no contingency of the actual, no unintelligibility of what is merely given."[7] Gadamer's argument, pointed out the path to the pursuit of art to the interpretation of the law, the legal norms and the spirit of law and the art of adjudication for us: in the purpose of pursuing aesthetic and artistic realm, for all art, whether it is literature, music and art, poetry or dance, would cultivate people's mind. The enjoyment of art and beauty is not only a form of sensibility, but also a kind of intellectual sustenance. True art and beauty do not have to say, do not have to appreciate, do not have to experience, it is devoting, it is melting, and it is the integration of people and the realm of the object, and this integration is exactly the pursuit of the law.

Some scholar believes that the law is not an expedient measure of human social interaction, but the necessity of orderly human communication. Furthermore, the law is the norm of human social structure, the crystallization of the wisdom of law lies in its spirit of coordination. "Law is the basis for human beings to keep order, safety, freedom, efficiency and justice, is the result of repeated representations, games and choices. The structure of the social system can not be away from the law. Law is not only the product of the ultimate concern of human beings, but also the symbol of ultimate concern. Law is an essential element of human life, orderly life, free communication and eternal guardian."[8] This understanding is not only different from the author's interpretation of law, legal spirit and the judge's art of trial, but also quite common.

In my personal view, the law is the embodiment of human beauty and happiness values, and the law is the norm for the pursuit of nature and human being. The law is the collective power used to raise the happiness index of mankind. The real value of law is the happiness of human society. The ultimate reason of law is the imbalance and the lack of distribution of social welfare. Happiness is the origin of aesthetics and art. The art of adjudication is the professional skill of pursuing the aesthetics of

[6]Hans-Georg Gadamer, Aesthetics and Hermeneutics, Translated by David E. Linge, see http://www.thinkingtogether.org/rcream/archive/old/S2005/127/gadamer.pdf.

[7]Hans-Georg Gadamer, Aesthetics and Hermeneutics, Translated by David E. Linge, see http://www.thinkingtogether.org/rcream/archive/old/S2005/127/gadamer.pdf.

[8]Xie [6].

legal spirit and the realm of art. What we pursue is not pure beauty, is not a simple happiness, but a kind of conformity with the law of beauty and the realization of multi-level integration of the realm of happiness, is a kind of aesthetic interpretation. Therefore, it is a kind of virtue, and also a kind of good deeds for the judge to take the judicial profession as an art. I agree with Posner said, "Law is an art, but also a mystery."[9] I would like to interpret the mystery as a kind speculation about beauty before the "unknown" and the enlightenment of happiness after the "known".

The interpretation of the law, the spirit of the law and the art of adjudication in the book may be different from other interpretation methods, but may be precise because of the different perspectives, there would be different effects of "harmony but not sameness". No matter how big the difference, it is necessary to identify: since ancient times, the decryption of the law, the legal norms and the judiciary has never been stopped, the relevant theories are always changing and developing, there is no dogmatic truth, but only eternal dialogue and interpretation.[10] I hope my understanding can find the truth of one of its points, and open the window of the beauty for the well-being of people.

2 An Analysis on the Values of Law and the Art of Adjudication

The study of legal value has become the basic category of law. On the meaning of legal value, different scholars have different views. Professor Li Long believes that the legal value is the property that the law satisfies the needs of the subject based on its own regulations. The legal value is an independent proposition of legal philosophy, and it can not be separated from the representation and realization of the legal system; meanwhile it is restricted and guided by the legal values.[11] Professor Xie Pengcheng argues that legal value is the subordination relationship of law to the subject, formed in the way of the subject promoting the law to adapt to and submit to the internal scale of the subject through the understanding, evaluation and legal practices. This subordinate relationship is not a priori or conscious field, but the subject actively and dynamically acting on the law and the law acting on the subject in the legal practice, is an objective fact.[12] Professor Zhang Wenxian argues that the legal value is the unity of social and class nature, the unity of subjectivity and objectivity, the unity of relativity and absoluteness, the unity of purpose value and means value; order, justice, freedom and benefit are the basic value of laws.[13] Roscoe Pound wrote in his book "*Social Control Through Law*", the problem of values is one from which the science of law cannot escape. In the classical eras of legal history, both in the ancient

[9]Posner [7].

[10]Xie [6], p. 602.

[11]Li [8].

[12]Xie [9].

[13]Zhang [10].

and in the modern world, demonstration or criticism or logical application of such canons of value have been among the chief activities of jurists.[14] The value of law is intrinsic, inexperienced, abstract value; it is the essence value and behind the law; it is the value that can be perceived indirectly through the characteristics of the law, especially the operation and the result of the law, and it is the true manifestations of human nature. Man's understanding of the value of law can only be approached, and can not reach an end. The debate on the knowledge and understanding of legal value becomes the eternal subject of human pursuit of legal significance. Legal values are the psychological state of people's knowledge, understanding and adaption of legal value, including the two aspects of perceptual knowledge and rational knowledge, the specific performance: people's knowledge, understanding, needs of the legal value and so on.

I believe that the legal value which guides the judge's judicial art should be the value of good law, should be the legal value unified by the truth, goodness and beauty of the law as the standard, and should be the legal value seeking public welfare concept for the human society. Values determine the behavior of the judge, the judge's role is played under the guidance and influence of values, what kind of values will have what kind of judgment. Therefore, the value plays an important role in the art of adjudication.

The right standard model of modern law guides the return of humanistic spirit, so that it becomes the essential factor of modern legal spirit, and becomes the starting point of studying legal value. Humane spirit is a set of concept system, also is a kind of lofty idea. Its essence is: everything from the needs of human beings, human-centered, regarding human as the subject of idea, behavior and system; human emancipation and freedom, human dignity, happiness and all-round development, should become the ultimate concern of individuals, community, society and government; individuals and groups as a subject, should have self-consciousness of justice, tolerance, honesty, self-reliance, self-improvement, self-discipline. Humanistic spirit is characterized by the promotion of human subjectivity and value, equal respect and care for human rights.[15] Market economy and civil society are the original of humanistic spirit, the humanistic spirit is developed based on the civil society and civil culture, and the true, the good and the beauty of law is another expression of the humanistic spirit. The essence of beauty, the true meaning of beauty, the law of beauty and the feeling of happiness are the value forms of human spirit. The overall progress of today's society can not be separated from the humanistic spirit, building a harmonious society can not be separated from the humanistic spirit, which is the profound connotation of modern legal values. Therefore, the adjudication art should be the legal value constructed on the foundation of modern humanism, which is the connotation of the value of the adjudication art, the necessity of modern legal development, the inspiration of the value of good law, the value of the truth, the good, and the beauty, and the value of happiness followed by the judge's judicial art. Under the guidance of the humanism, the ultimate purpose of the adjudication is to realize the double freedom of human

[14]Pound [11].

[15]Zhang [10], pp. 389–390.

behavior and spirit by establishing an orderly and equal relationship between rights and obligations.

3 Pragmatic Jurisprudence and the Art of Adjudication

Pragmatism, which originated in the United States in the late nineteenth century, is one of the most influential schools of Philosophy in contemporary America. The formation of pragmatism in the United States is not accidental, as an immigrant country, pragmatism had some affinity with the emerging country, and it has profound social and historical roots. Since the beginning of pragmatism, it has had a great impact on the emerging country, so to speak, it involves all aspects of American society, known as the "American spirit"". In the book *The Common Law*, Justice Holmes put forward the idea that "the life of the law has been experienced", and emphasized the new meaning of the precedent on the basis of respecting the historical tradition, which laid the foundation for the emergence of pragmatism jurisprudence.[16]

Justice Holmes is the first person to combine the theory of historical jurisprudence and the theory of utilitarian analysis jurisprudence, established the theory of context and instrumentalism approach. Cardozo applied this approach to judicial practice, deepening the theory of "judge-made law" in the judicial process. At that time, the trial of some cases was deeply marked by the brand of "legal pragmatism".[17] The pragmatic theory of law has a very important guidance and reference for the theoretical construction of the judge's trial art, which is the important theoretical basis of the judge's trail art in the modern sense. The art of adjudication is shining the light of the wisdom of pragmatism jurisprudence. Holmes believed that in the process of forming a precedent, compared with the deductive reasoning, the needs of the times felt by the people, and popular moral idea and political theory, recognized or unconscious intuitive knowledge of public policy, even the judge's prejudice shared with his contemporaries, and these open or unconscious factors played the greater role. The law embodies the history of the development of a nation for centuries, so it cannot be regarded as a mathematical textbook that includes only principles and theorems. It is true that legal logic is the essence of case law. However, this kind of logic is not syllogism in formal logic, but the logic based on the experience. Holmes jumped out of the framework of the analysis of the law, but connected the law with politics, economy, morality, history, psychology and many other factors, emphasizing the essence of the law has been the practical subjective experience.[18] The "experience" Holmes said refers to the judges in accordance with the premise of precedent, according to the changes in the social life, give precedent to a new life.[19]

---

[16]Miao [12].

[17]Miao [12].

[18]Miao [12], p. 46.

[19]Miao [12], p. 46.

To a large extent, the composition theory of the adjudication art is very similar with the theory of pragmatism, and the adjudication art emphasizes a lot on "experience", believing the experience is the accumulation of judge's wisdom, the existing judicial experience can be based on the new case of the new situation and flexible application. Empiricism is also a pragmatism in a sense.

The foundation of case law is Stare Decisis, which means that the judge should consider the legal principles and rules contained in the previous similar case judgment of the superior court or the court. The precedent is binding. For legal philosophy, Holmes emphasized that the vitality of law had been the experience, it means asking people to adapt to the needs of the times based on the respect of common law history, and to modify or supplement the old legal system.[20] Although our country is not a case law country, but many cases still have some reference to the handling of other cases, the guiding value, in a certain sense, is still the prototype of "Stare Decisis"; with the development of social life, the understanding of the written code also continue to deepen and develop, the "experience" of the judge's trial is also getting a new life when applied to the new case. Thus, although pragmatism jurisprudence arises from the United States, which has the case law as the main source of law, many theories of pragmatism can still be introduced to China's judges' judicial art. Many aspects of the art of adjudication can learn and use the substantive content of the theory of pragmatic jurisprudence to summarize and improve.

Cardozo elaborated on the role of judges in the judicial process, he was the first modern justice who told people how he judged and how he made law, his enduring reputation in the American legal profession stems from his deep insight into the methods of judgment. In his famous book, "The Nature of the Judicial Process", Cardozo elaborated on the concept of "judge-made law". He believed that when the judge heard a case, there were four kinds of methods: (1) The directive force of a principle may be exerted along the line of logical progression; this I will call the rule of analogy or the method of philosophy; (2) along the line of historical development; this I will call the method of evolution; (3) along the line of the customs of the community; this I will call the method of tradition; (4) along the lines of justice, morals and social welfare, the mores of the day; and this I will call the method of sociology.[21] The analysis of the nature of the judicial process by Justice Cardozo has important theoretical and practical significance for the improvement of the level of the adjudication art. Judges should accurately locate their professional role, according to the nature of the judicial process to choose different adjudication methods.

As to the boundary of the judge-made law, Justice Cardozo said, "If you ask how he is to know when one interest outweighs another, I can only answer that he must get his knowledge just as the legislator gets it, from experience and study and reflection; in brief, from life itself. Here, indeed, is the point of contact between the legislator's work and his. The choice of methods, the appraisement of values, must in the end be guided by like considerations for the one as for the other. Each indeed is legislating within the limits of his competence. No doubt the limits for the judge are narrower.

[20] Miao [12], pp. 69–70.

[21] Cardozo [13].

He legislates only between gaps. He fills the open spaces in the law. How far he may go without traveling beyond the walls of the interstices cannot be staked out for him upon a chart."[22] Although our country is not a case law country, the function of the judge to make law is not inferior to the case law country, the judge as long as unwilling to just be a "law craftspeople", his/her "law-making" fields and spaces are quite broad. Based on the principle that the judge must not refuse to judge, in the absence of specific provisions of the law, the judge would have to make a decision based on the principles and the spirit of the law, morality and habits; in the process of applying the laws, In the event of conflicting laws or loopholes in the law, the judge should also choose the best legal norms, make up for legal loopholes, and creatively apply the law; in the process of resolving disputes, when the judge discovers that the law is incompatible with other social governance structures or the use of legal means is difficult to achieve the ultimate goal, it can be remedied by means of judicial advice. These are actually "making the law", just our judge-made law has different forms from that of the case law country. "Judge-making law" is an important skill in the judges' trail, and the theory of "judge-made law" in pragmatism can be one of the important theoretical basis for creatively applying the law of Chinese judges.

4 Legal Culture and the Art of Adjudication

The interpretation of legal culture, from the perspective of Professor Liu Zuoxiang, can be understood from two perspectives, which are the legal culture as a methodology and the legal culture as an object. "Legal culture" is a kind of thinking mode and research method to understand the legal phenomenon with the view of culture, also a kind of cultural structure with substance content and objectification, and these two aspects are related to each other.[23] Law is a kind of culture, which embodies the wisdom, knowledge and experience of the people to adjust the social relations. As a part of the superstructure, the law should not exclude the content of culture. Legal culture is the crystallization of human wisdom and spiritual wealth created by legal practice in the long history of human society and the cultural foundation of the existence and development of social and legal phenomenon.[24]

The art of adjudication is closely related to legal culture. The construction of art is bound to have a profound cultural heritage, and the adjudication art can be called art because it's inseparable with the legal culture. In the modern sense, the art of adjudication actually incorporates our traditional legal culture and western legal culture, which is the product of the combination of Chinese and western legal culture. As far as the reality is concerned, the Chinese judge's trial is influenced by two legal cultures, one is the infiltration of Chinese culture and the other is the western culture. Being placed in the cultural background of two kinds of legal cultures intertwined, the

[22] Cardozo [13], 1921, pp. 112–113.

[23] Liu [14].

[24] Liu [14], p. 93.

thought, the idea and the professional skill of the judge is a kind of integration of the Chinese and Western culture. The integration of the two cultures not only provides a richer ideological resource and theoretical basis, but also poses a severe challenge for the development of the adjudication art, and puts forward the higher practice quality and ability claim of the judge. On the one hand, the Chinese judges grew up under the background of Chinese traditional culture, and the traditional Chinese culture, especially the traditional legal culture, laid a deep imprint on the thoughts and ideas of the judges. On the other hand, because our modern legal system is basically transplanted, the western legal thought and legal culture within the western legal system also spread to China with the transplant of the legal system, which profoundly influenced the construction of the judicial system and the style of the judge's trial. At present, China's judicial system reform is based on learning and drawing on western legal thoughts and legal culture. However, according to the viewpoint of Professor Fan Zhongxin, Chinese nearly a hundred years of "Legal Westernization" Movement, there are many overcorrect deficiency; the "overcorrect" legal reform has made our legal system not only overly confront the Chinese cultural tradition, but also deviate from the spiritual tradition of the western law culture. Many systems established since modern times, especially since the founding of People's Republic of China, have actually cut off their own two umbilicals: one is the umbilical cord of Chinese traditional legal culture and the other is the civil law system. After cutting off the umbilical cord, the systems failed to grow and develop independently, making people feel strange, diaphragm, and alienated. A new legal system that merged the essence of western legal civilization and Chinese legal tradition hasn't come into being, which is the embarrassment of our legal system today.[25] I believe that the role of judges in the reconstruction of modern legal culture and the adjustment of the legal system is enormous, and the judicial activities of the professional judge group are actually a reflection of legal culture. Judging from the perspective of legal culture, advocating the judge's trial art is actually advocating a kind of Chinese modern legal culture which meets the needs of the new era. To a large extent, the formation of the modern legal culture is closely related to the collective efforts of judges, and to a large extent depends on the formation and development of the adjudication art. Meanwhile, the adjudication art is deeply influenced by the legal culture, and it also shows certain legal cultural characteristics, is a bridge between legal culture and social reality. The deep commonality in the Chinese and western legal culture traditions requires the professional judges' groups to seek and explain in the process of utilizing the art of adjudication.

The background of the law is the culture and the society, and the legal system is the social image of politics, economics, religion, ethics and other cultural achievements. Any era, any style or form of civilization has its ethical core. Ethic is the soul of civilization. The legal system of any nation actually exists to protect these ethics from being trampled or abandoned. The law of traditional Chinese society is the typical representative of this kind of law. China's traditional legal culture thought is mainly Confucian culture, and as to China traditional society, undergoing two

---

[25]Zhongxin [15].

thousand years of governance and chaos alternated, there has been a formation of the legislative culture, which is the unsophisticated etiquette and ethical of the law. On the one hand, turning the ethical principles into law in the way of "not distinguishing ceremony and law", "introducing ceremony into law", and "combining ceremony and law"; on the other hand, safeguarding the prestige and effectiveness of "ceremony" in the ways of "punishing all demeanors that violate the ceremony" and "morality given priority over penalty". These two approaches are very successful in strengthening the ethics of the spiritual pillar of a civilized order, especially for the strengthening of the economic order of the patriarchal clan of "being harmonious and respect".[26] In addition, the system of Confucian ethics is emphasized clan and class, emphasizing the maintenance of arithmetic and orderly society, emphasizing the construction of a harmonious society of "moral standard". Among the China traditional legal culture, the legal operation of the society is quite diverse, the legal functions of the organizations, clans, guilds and neighborhood, have played a role, patriarchal, rules, local customs and other living laws play a more active role than national law. The rural society of China is an "anti-litigation society", because of believing in "peace is most precious", even it was the surface harmony, it was better than the actual open conflict.[27] China's national law is based on the highest moral, and the folk law is based on the habit of morality. From the point of view of the essence of law, both the national law and the folk law are strongly influenced by Confucian ethics. Confucian ideal society is such kind of society, where there are great or small, seniors and juniors, old and young, close and distant, on the foundation of human relationship (natural social relations), there has been interacting with each other. The five cardinal relationships are a summary of naturally occurring social relations: father and son have relatives, monarch and justice righteousness, young and old seniority, friends faith.[28] Confucian ethics has become a major force through the great and little traditions, not only in the great tradition has great impact on the ritual classics and the codes, and restricts the emperor, literati and officialdom and other ruling classes behavior; by the influence of gentlemen, people following the example of their superiors, the Confucianism goes to the people, combined with the customs of little tradition, becomes the norm of daily life.[29] After a long period of development, Confucian ethics in China society has become the primary specification of the social relationship, even in today's society, Confucian ethics is still a mainstream tradition of legal culture, can be seen everywhere in the traces of the adjustment of the operating process of modern social relationships. The legal culture under the guidance of Confucian ethics is the local legal and cultural resources of modern Chinese judges' trial art. It is an important source of theoretical reference. Chinese judges should absorb the essence of the legal culture in the process of adjudication. This will not only help the judge to deepen the understanding of the historical meaning of the

[26]Zhongxin [16].

[27]Lin [17].

[28]Lin [17], p. 10.

[29]Lin [17], p. 16.

law itself, but also help to understand the role of the professional judicial skill, and promote the application and development of the adjudication art in the real society.

From ancient Greece to modern times, western legal culture and legal thought are also beneficial to the construction of the rule of the law society in China. Especially, the modern judicial concepts such as freedom, equality, justice, justice and procedure in western legal culture have a great guiding effect on the adjudication art. The most deficient of the vocational skills of modern Chinese judges is the integration of modern judicial ideas and traditional legal culture. The rule of law promoting is not born in the traditional Chinese culture, but learned from the civilization of the Western society. The constitution of the late Qing Dynasty and the legal reform by Shen Jiaben was the first time that China had absorbed the western legal culture, not only absorbed the legal technology, but also introduced the judicial ideas and the legal culture. The process of the reform of the judicial culture in modern China is a conflict process of the traditional judicial culture and the western judicial culture. It is also the process that Chinese traditional judicial culture abandoned itself and realized the transformation of creation.[30] In the modern sense, many contents of the judge's trial art are inspired by the modern judicial ideas in the western legal culture. Advocating the adjudication art, from the perspective of western legal culture, is to improve the judicial skills by learning from the western legal cultures which are already existed, in accordance with the rule of law, and in line with the requirements of social progress, mainly the modern judicial idea. Modern judicial idea is the pursuit of human reason of natural law thought, is the ideological basis of justice system of the western rule of law society, and also an important connotation of western legal culture. It can be used to transform the original Chinese backward law and the legal system, the essence of western legal culture can be used by borrowlism; or can be combined the western legal culture with the national conditions of China, to develop and innovate into a new legal culture, filling in more cultural information for the rule of law in China. The judge's trail should pay attention not only to absorb the essence of western legal culture, but also to combine western legal culture and Chinese traditional legal culture, and strive to make the combine of the modern western legal culture and Chinese local cultural resources produce the cultural connotation of the adjudication art.

5 Public Relations and the Art of Adjudication

Public relations is a social organization or individual in operation to make themselves and the public mutual understanding, mutual cooperation and the dissemination of activities and the behavior norms. It includes the following meanings: (1) public relations is a kind of social relations, the relationships between social organizations and the public; among them, the social organization is the subject and the public is the object. (2) public relations is a kind of communication activity. The link between social organizations and the public is the communication activity, which has a certain

[30]E-xiang [18].

behavioral norm, so as to ensure its normal and effective work. (3) public relations is a kind of information communication. There is a two-way exchange of information between social organizations and the public, and the social organizations continue to release information to the public, and obtain feedback from the public. (4) public relations have certain control functions, in a sense, the social organizations is a control system, which can adjust their behavior and norms at any time according to the feedback information to, in order to further exchanges and cooperation for the public. (5) public relations is a purposeful activity. Public relations as a communication activity has clear purpose, that is to make the social organizations and the public mutual to achieve mutual understanding and mutual cooperation, the social organization to establish a good image in front of the public, and have common interests with the public. (6) public relations is a kind of relationship, a kind of technique, a kind of professional skills which turns the " thought of letting their own development make others also get material benefits and efficiency" into practice. (7) public relations is a kind of cultural phenomenon in modern society. "Respect, understanding, support and cooperation" is the basic concept of this kind of cultural phenomenon. (8) public relations is a profession, is a kind of occupation to maintain a harmonious and stable relationship between social organizations and the public. Connecting the public relations and the adjudication art is the practical need for the court's trial work. To a certain extent, the art of adjudication is good public relations, setting up the consciousness of public relations is the methods and ways to improve the art of adjudication.

Public relations is the product of the development of modern society, and the development of public relations is constantly promoting the development of modern society. In this sense, the research and application of public relations is of great practical significance. As for the judicial art, the practical significance of public relations in the judicial art lies in: China is currently in the primary stage of socialism and the period of social transformation, and the country is speeding up the process of legalization; The legal culture dominated by Confucian ethics for thousands of years is colliding strongly with the western legal culture tradition. The social background requires the judicial work of the People's Courts and the modern art of adjudication should be adapt to the realistic national conditions, social conditions and sentiments, and get out of the conservative, stubborn and backward thought cages, seeking dialogue way.

The laws of all countries in the world are used to regulate the complex interests, but relatively speaking, the interests adjusted by the law of contemporary China have special complexity. The complexity stems from the following aspects of reality: first, China is a large population and vast territory of the multi-ethnic country, the ecological environment and natural resources are not superior, the economic and cultural development is unbalanced, East and West, North and South, urban and rural areas, the regional disparity is large. The imbalance between the integrity of the people's court's adjudication work and the uniformity of legal application and the situation of national conditions requires special coordination through extroverted public relations. Secondly, China is in the primary stage of socialism, the social productivity is relatively backward, the market economy is undeveloped. Under such conditions, the construction of socialism must go through a special accumulation stage. The trial work of the people's courts must be adapted to the special requirements of the primary stage, to understand and to serve the special needs of the public in the particular period. The popularization and application of public relations will help the judge to observe the special needs of the public and make the judicial level to meet the needs of the society. Thirdly, China is now in a period of social transformation, the ongoing economic reform and political reform would inevitably touch some vested interests, and to break the various interests formed too. The conflicts of interests among the state, the collective and the individual, the disputes of interests within and among the regions, departments, industries, enterprises, individuals, the conflicts between the majority and the minority, the long-term and the short-term, the entirety and the part are increasingly intensified. The inherent patterns of various economic interests are gradually falling apart under the impact of the new interests, and the distribution of interests is characterized by diversity, dispersion and mobility. Meanwhile, as the economic transformation period has not yet formed a perfect market economy system and a strong macro-control mechanism, the legal system construction is still in the process of exploration and perfection, which determines our reform is inevitably full of contradictions. The conflicts which cannot be reconciled through economic means would finally resort to the judiciary. When facing the complicated conflicts of interests, only by means of rigid regulation of law cannot meet the needs of reality, the judges must make full use of public relations, a flexible, indirect, slightly modest adjustment, to solve the problem with softness and strength. Finally, the reforms in the social transformation period have had a strong impact on the traditional values and customary forces of the past and have spawned new ideas and new ways of thinking. Besides, we do not deny that the reform has brought a byproduct of extreme individualism, money worship, hedonism and abnormal and destructive psychological factors. It is bound to exacerbate the conflict of interests and undermine social stability and harmony. The court is the last line of defense of social fairness, the judges must adjust and balance these complex conflicts of interest through judicial means, fully study and use the various skills and methods of public relations, and break through the limitations of realistic conditions and achieve the best results. If the judge can pay attention to the use of public relations, will enable the court and the people to achieve two-way information exchange and communication, let the public to better understand and support the court's trial work, so that the court can be displayed an open, fair and impartial image in front of the community. In this sense, public relations is one level of adjudication art.

Public relations and the judge's judicial art are complementary. With the deepening of the reform of trial mode and judicial system, it is more and more important to cultivate the public relations consciousness of judges. The judge must consider the relationship between case handling and the general will. Coordinating the relationship between the judge and the general will is also an important content of the judge's judicial art. We refer to the public relations that judges use public relations as judicial public relations.

Along with the progress and development of the whole society, and the dissemination of new ideas and new knowledge, modern social public presents new psychological characteristics: Independent awareness is generally enhanced, group communication is increasingly active, extensive and in-depth, the spontaneous activities of the public have formed a potential, independent social forces, its energy and power is enough to confront social organizations, the media repeatedly reported violent anti-law event is the best example is the result of the combination of the state of mind and the spontaneous movement of the public. The best example is the law-enforcing events reported by the medias, and the results of the combination of the mentality of "the law does not punish the public" and the force of the public spontaneous activity. In modern society, the public are welcome and cooperative to the judicial public relations, the judges' the emphasis on public relations in a certain extent is to respect the existence value of public, applying the public relations can coordinate and balance the relationship between the court and the public, which is beneficial to the unity of the legal effect and social effect. The establishment of democratic politics laid the foundation for the development of judicial public relations. The highly-developed market economy provided the realistic soil for the application of the judicial public relations, and the rapid development of modern communication technology provided the technical means for the large-scale practice of public relations.

The judicial public relations in the development of modern society has a profound philosophical basis. From the macroscopic aspect, the judicial public relations is a kind of legal culture phenomenon in modern society. From the microscopic aspect, the judicial public relations is one of the values of the adjudications according to law. The judicial public relations is actually a kind behaving guidance in the process of the adjudication, is the modern judges necessary vocational skills and quality requirements, is the civilized procedures of the communication between the modern judges and the public. From the meso-level aspect, the judicial public relations is the necessary lubricant in the whole process of modern society. Judges use this rigid means of law to adjust the various relations of rights and obligations, the judicial public relations is needed as the buffer, lubrication and coordination in order to achieve the best results.

For the development of modern society, the judge's advocating the harmony of public relations in the process of adjudication is the mass line of the new era. It is the inheritance and development of the fine tradition of the mass line through profession behavior by the judge. It is the sublation of the mass line by the judicial reform. Mass line is our traditional judicial experience, is the basis of traditional judicial work. "Close contact with the masses, from the masses, to the masses" has been the Party's work methods. However, there is a certain degree of contradiction and conflict between the reform content established by modern judicial idea and pleading trial mode and the traditional mass line in idea and form. The judges going deep into the masses, investigating and studying, fully soliciting the views of the masses, handling the cases based on extensive investigation and research, focusing on the social effect of the judgments, these are the successes of the "Ma Xi-wu trial mode" in the past judicial practice, which was in accordance with the special historical conditions at that time. It can be said that the mass line is one of the successful experiences of the traditional justice, and the magic weapon of judicial success in socialist revolution; but in the new historical conditions, the mass line must derive the new meaning so as to extend to new living space. The judicial public relations is the application of the mass line in the trial work in the new era. Its functions include: (1) Monitoring function. Judges use the judicial public relations to continuously collect, process and feedback information to keep abreast of changes in the internal and external circumstances of the court, to test the status of the judiciary of the court and the realization of the task of trial work, but also through a variety of information media feedback to detect and grasp the attitude of the litigants and the public on the courts and the judges trial, to prevent the unforeseen circumstances of the court and the judges. (2) Cohesion function. The judicial public relations is an art of "seeking internal unite and seeking external development", and the cohesion function of judicial public relations can make the negative effect of the internal friction and separation tendency inside the court constantly change to the positive effect, so that not only the judges and the trial organizations in the courts can work together and operate normally, but also the development of the courts can obtain a wider range of external support. (3) Regulation function. In the process of exercising the judicial power independently, the court will inevitably have friction with the object. The adjustment function of the judicial public relations has the function of reducing the friction coefficient, effectively avoiding the occurrence or intensification of the contradiction, and achieving the preventive effect, to minimize the possibility of the harm to the individual judges and the court, so as to form the harmonious relationships of mutual understanding and mutual cooperation among the court, the judge and the public. (4) Strain function. When the image of the court or the judge is damaged, when the relations among the court, the judge and the public are destroyed, the utilization of the judicial public relations can actively resist and respond to change this bad situation, and the situation can be improved.

In a country with a sound legal system, judge profession is a lonely profession, and judges are cautious judges. The judge communicates with the public with his/her impartial adjudication. In the context of our country, judges should also be cautious in speech and behavior, but discretion in speech and behavior does not conflict with the judicial public relations. On the contrary, being cautious in speech and behavior are parallel to the judicial public relations and are both part of the adjudication art. The judicial public relations is a kind of judicial transmission mode adopted by courts and judges in their daily work in order to make mutual understanding and mutual cooperation with the public. This kind of behavior includes the mode of "being cautious in speech" and "being cautious in behavior". The court and the judge must disseminate their actual performance to the public in an appropriate manner, which requires a good carrier. One kind of carrier is the legal system propaganda and the judicial information dissemination, which is the tangible propaganda; another kind is judge's behavior in the trial. Judges' "being cautious in speech" and "being cautious in behavior" in the trial itself is "advertising", a kind of invisible propaganda. Although the coverage of intangible propaganda is limited, the subtle influence is far-reaching. A good image of the judge's cautious speech and behavior and noble personality charm will infect the people around, if supplemented by tangible propaganda to expand the effect of intangible propaganda, the art of adjudication will be widely known, and the charm of justice will be recognized.

6 Multiple Thought of the Art of Adjudication

I. The art of adjudication and the politics

The judicial adjudication should belong to the cross-field of political science and jurisprudence. At the macro level, it involves the institutional, organizational, role and other structural and functional areas, should be the subject of political science; at the micro level, it involves the legal method and the legal procedure and the judicial professional skill application areas, should belong to the subject of jurisprudence. When we discussing the judge's judicial art, we should consider the political factors of it, and the theoretical construction of judge's judicial art should have the content of political science; in a country such as China, there's no doubt that the judge's judicial art contains the content of political art, it is necessary to open up the political view. In essence, since modern times, the development of Chinese judicial structure is nothing more than a part of Chinese political development. Therefore, lack of research from the perspective of politics will certainly make the theory lack of distribution.[31] We explore the judicial structure of the judge's professional skills also need to learn from the theoretical nutrients of political science.

As we have mentioned in the previous chapter, judicature is a common political phenomenon in political society, and is a structure in the political system that exists in the political society. As a legal certification, judicature acts as a powerful tool for the political power in the superstructure, and when protecting public opinion, it spares no effort to reflect the political needs at the same time. The judicature is actually the operating power in a specific political background, never get rid of the political haze, nor go beyond the political level to try the pure rule of law. This is the basic relationship between the judicial and political systems. Accordingly, the judge's judicial system is the social adjustment method under the political system, the judge's trial is restricted by the political atmosphere; leaving the field and the scope of politics, the social function of the adjudication art would be weakened.

The adjudication art in the modern sense should accord with the inherent logic of modern political development. The outcome of modern political development is the constitutional theory and model. In modern times, constitutionalism is the dominant form of democratic politics, to sum up its basic value is to maintain and develop human dignity and rights through the regulation of government power.[32] The core of constitutionalism lies in the translation of political issues into legal issues, to regulate the power of the government in the form of the Constitution and the law,

[31]Zhuru [19].

[32]Zhuru [19], p. 52.

through the legal institutionalization of the way, so that the actual operation of political power is conducive to the maintenance and promotion of human dignity and the realization of rights, to truly realize the people's sovereignty and basic human rights. The importance of judicature in modern politics comes from the form of constitutionalism of modern politics. Judicial judicature and judgments are also based on constitutionalism, and take the civilization form pursued by the constitutionalism as ideal. The art of adjudication is the professional art and political art under the request of constitutionalism. Judge in the process of judging the problem is to complete a certain political mission, the relevant vocational skills also expressed as a political art; judges in the adjudication process concern about the political background of the law and its harmonious relationship of the constitutional system, is self-consciousness and self-adaptation of social responsibility. Understandably, judges have never been judged in political vacuum, no matter how independent the judiciary will have more or less political nature, influenced by the mainstream political consciousness, even in the developed rule of law countries, and the political bias of the justice happens in the adjudication if it is hidden. Therefore, the art of adjudication is the behavioral art and ideological art that is dominated by specific political civilization, and often unconsciously become the silhouette of the politics. It is futile for the judge to completely break away from the political science to talk about art, and the necessary political connotation is a deep understanding of the relationship between law and politics.

II. The art of adjudication and religion

Law and religion are two very closely related categories. The law restricts the future with its stability, and the religion challenges all existing social structures with its sacred ideas. At the same time, law and religion interpenetrate each other. Both in the subject features include the understanding of nature and society, the recognition of life and rights, the ideal of the future and love, although the source of power is not the same, but have different degrees of coercion, and have inner basis. From the perspective of mutual relations, a society's ultimate belief of transcendence purpose would definitely manifest itself in the process of adjusting the social order, and the legal adjustment process of the social order would also be seen in its consciousness of the ultimate purpose. In fact, in some societies, the law is the religious doctrines, such as the Five Books of Moses of ancient Israel. Even in those societies that strictly distinguished law and religion, law and religion have never been separated. The law gives the religion with the sociality, the religion gives the law with the spiritual direction, causing the law to have mystique, which makes people fascinated, deeply awesome.

Therefore, law and religion are interlinked, and there are something that can be used for reference. As far as the judge's trial is concerned, it is necessary for the judge to absorb the spiritual connotation of religion, and to construct the life of art with the help of the sacred power of religious spirit and the firm power of holding the faith. First of all, the loyalty of judges to law, should be the same as the faith of believers to religion. The law delineates the boundaries of citizenship and the limits of the power of the magistrate. Overstepping the boundaries of the citizen must be punished by the law, exceeding the power of the judge must be blamed by the system and tortured by the faith. Judges should always be based on the will of the law, the social interests, political needs, public order, fine custom, and moral traditions should be established on the principle of rule of law. Secondly, the process of the judicial art is the process of the integration of legal value and religious value. The artistic spirit of the judge's trial lies in the fact that the judges, through their superb judicial skills, evolve the zeal of religious beliefs into the spirit of law and, at the same time, through the normative and universal role of the law evolving into a similar religious inner power, making the law and religion to play a role in different space-time, together constitute the rational norms of human society, acting on the human soul. There is an old saying in China, "there are national laws one chi overhead, there are gods three chi overhead", is the best expression of the relationship between law and religion, which proves that the ancients have begun to seek the intersection of law and religion in the unknown world, and have had a deeper understanding, religious holy doctrine has even become a great support for the law.

Law is one aspect of love and faith. Without love and faith, a law is not really law. It is because of love and faith that law is the basis for human beings to be respected. The art of adjudication lies in the fact that the judge embodies the love and belief of the law in the course of the case trial, which allows the litigants and the public to experience the rationality and warmth of the law. The reason why God's law, God's judgment is a wonderful thing, a noble and joyful thing, is that it is considered to practice happiness, bring the comfort of the soul, and reach a real understanding between people.

China is a special religious belief pattern in which Buddhism, Taoism and Confucianism coexist, among which Confucian ethics have the most profound influence on Chinese legal culture. The traditional Confucian, heavy ceremony light law, has now left us the brand of restraining law and belittling litigation, and applying the law arbitrarily. The judicature often gives the impression of a mechanical, cold, narrow and rigid, and it is hard to tell how much the sheriff loved his job and how loyal he was to the law. Therefore, the modern judicial trial should combine the spiritual essence of the traditional Confucianism and the pious faith of the supremacy of law, and cultivate the spirit of abiding by the law and the courage of enforcing the law.

III. The art of adjudication and literature

Law and literature have a natural affinity. From the formal point of view, both law and literature are expressed in words, the common law countries record the law in judgments and the civil law countries turning the legal will in print in the form of Codex; the legal language emphasizes grammaticality, accuracy, readiness, and literary expression is more complicated, but simple and easy to understand, easy to communicate is the basic requirements of the general form of literature. From the content point of view, it is full of ideas, spirit, and value in the plain legal text, and it is reflected the author's thoughts and likes and dislikes in the various forms of literary works, pursuing a certain social effect, and exchanging thoughts and sympathy. If we weaken the mandatory and violent characteristics of the law, if we explore the social soil of legal growth, we will find that law reveals the truth of real life or try to reveal the truth of real life as literature. In this sense, the law is actually a literary work with multiple emotional qualities, although it does not show the exaggerated words and jokes, but borrows basic literary techniques such as narration, description and description.

The judicature is the running process of law, and the adjudication is the activation of law. In the judicial process, judges make the literary nature of the law coruscate, and in the judgment documents, show the literary accomplishment. The adjudication's literature has a long history in our country. One of the salient features of the ancient judgment is the pursuit of symmetry of the structure, the beauty of the text, the profound meaning, the ethics of the accessible, and the emotional abundance. The Su Shi's verdict of Song Dynasty is not so much a judgment as a literary art, which has a strong literary flavor and a unique beauty of the parallel prose, embodies the characteristics of the ancient judges' trial art. Today's adjudication has almost faded out of the literary style, and become formatted, public culture, simplification. The fixation and simplicity of the model reduced the requirement of the character, structure and aesthetic feeling of the adjudication, degenerating into simple official documents.

The adjudication art is largely dependent on the expression of the skills and methods of literature. The combination of law and literature is an important way to improve the art of adjudication. China's research on legal and literary theory was carried out late, and didn't have some research results until 1990s. On the one hand, through the legal text to study the theory of legal literature, such as He Weifang, Wang Shirong and other scholars on the literary theory of ancient verdicts; on the other hand, through the literature to study the theory of law and literature. Because the study of Chinese legal history is confined to the legal text, it is difficult to grasp the real situation of the ancient legal system and legal culture. Represented by Professor Xu Zhongming, legal history scholars began to break through the research fields and methods through the study of literature in the limitations of law, for example, researching the Criminal Procedure System of Song Dynasty by interpreting the Wu Song murdering Xi Menqing in the work "All Men Are Brothers". The scholars who study legal historiography try to regard the literary narrative of the law as a kind of material and way of interpreting our folk legal culture, because within the version, there are observations of the common people on social things, there are collective memories, there is a sense of legal awareness and the formation of legal consciousness of the ancient society, there are expressions of people's thoughts, feelings, wishes, there are reflections of legal effect. Theoretical study of some scholars, such as Su Li, Liang Zhiping, Liu Xing, study the theory of law and literature through the analysis of the legal stories in the literary works. Through the study of "The Story of Qiu Ju" and "The Accused Uncle Shan Gang", Professor Su Li described the embarrassing situation of the modern rule of law in China's rural areas, put forward the legal resources of the legal system, etc.

The art of adjudication to a certain extent belongs to the crossing field of law and literature, the theoretical research of law and literary should pay attention to the subject of adjudication art. In the long history, there are lots of examples of adjudication art. A nation's life creates its rule of law, and the jurist creates only the theory of the rule of law, and the litterateur interprets the soul of the rule of law. The litterateur's literary works are another interpretation of the legal spirit. The strained relation between the rules of life and the rules of law has never been well resolved and adequately cared for by the legal professionals, yet the litterateur has given instinctive, sufficient, and profound revelation. Concerned about the legal phenomenon in literature makes the legal professionals urgently feel that efforts should be made to try to establish a new type of jurisprudence, that is, proceeding from the reality of our legal life and the realistic problem of China's legal system, discover and refine the theoretical issues, exploring the rule of law in Chinese Context.[33] The theoretical study of law and literature should not ignore the theoretical exploration of the judge's trial, the art of adjudication is the professional judicial skills of the legal profession, but also a kind of art of life. We can also extract the theoretical problems with the legal significance of the adjudication art from legal texts and literary texts, pay attention to find the path and ways to improve and the professional skills of the judges, to seek a comprehensive upgrade the overall quality of judges and overall level of adjudication based on China's realistic.

Whether ancient or modern, at home and abroad, through the study of law and literature, we can feel the different skills and styles of judges in different times and different jurisdictions: for quotable good things, for pregnant aphorisms, for touchstones of ready application, the opinions of the English judges are a mine of instruction and a treasury of joy.[34] Such as Bai Juyi and Su Shi in ancient China, the court verdicts they wrote are just the same as proses, which are still popular and widely read today.

When the judge hears the cases, absorbing the connotation of the literature and art would make the handling of the case more in line with the concept of humanization of the law, so that the sensibility of human language can penetrate into the serious and rigid judicial activities, the professional skills of judges show more culture connotation and professional style; to make the judgments have the artistic temperament because of the literature; to make the public recognition and acceptance for the judicature having a more conscious composition, instead of being subject to the compulsory and arbitrary of the law. Leaving the nourishment of literary literacy, the legal text will become dry, the judicial process will become enervating, lack of life and people-concerned. Therefore, we advocate the literature of the judiciary, advocate the judges to strengthen the cultivation of literary literacy, and hope that through the infiltration of literary literacy, the judge's judicial art can become an elegant art in the sociological field.

IV. The art of adjudication and legal education

The art of adjudication is derived from the experience of judicial practice, but the basic part is derived from the technical training of legal theory and legal profession. Legal education should include two aspects: legal theory education and judicial vocational skills training. Since the restoration of the independent status in academic fields, law

[33]Tianjun [20].

[34]Cardozo [21].

has been developed into a famous school. In 1976, there were only two institutions to set up a law department around the country,[35] and now there are 425 institutions that opened a law school or law department. With the advancement of the rule of law and the speeding up of legislation, the legal theory has obtained a considerable development. The theory and practice have also been strengthened, and the teaching and research personnel have begun to form person echelon. Legal education has flourished.

However, from the perspective of judicial practice, there are still many problems in our legal education, of which the most prominent one is the negligence of the vocational education and training in our law school. So far, there is no prestigious institutions of law school officially set up the systematic judicial professional skills teaching courses, is still only the education of legal theory, lack of practical education; at most inviting judges and prosecutors to speech, sending students to the substantive departments to participate in internships, and the temporary practical course has not played its due role. Graduate students of Law School (including graduates, post-graduates, doctoral students) will take some time to meet the need of the post after a period of time, some even has always been difficult to adapt to the work of the judicial departments.

In modern legal education, theoretical knowledge and practical skills are still two separate areas. 425 institutions opened by the law school (department) can only master graduates with the knowledge of legal theory, legal education is more limited in the field of theoretical legal education. National Judges College, National Prosecutors College of P.R.C., Judges and prosecutors training centers (or Institute of Continuing Education) established by courts and procuratorates of all provinces and cities, are currently more engaged in special training and promotion training of judges and prosecutors, and there are no systematic professional judicial skills courses. Legal vocational skills education is now almost a blind spot in legal education. I believe that the current law undergraduate and law master education should lay a solid foundation for the judge's judicial art. In addition to the basic theoretical knowledge of law, in particular, education should pay attention to the cultivation of competencies, familiarize students with legal terminology and the basic theory of the law and the specific problems solved by the law, to help the students be able to conduct legal reasoning skillfully, so as to rely on the quality and basic knowledge of law education to quickly understand and apply the new law in the absence of classroom teaching.[36]

It is an urgent need to solve the problem that cultivating ability in the teaching of theoretical knowledge. Legal education should not only teach the knowledge of legal theory, but also how to analyze and apply the theoretical knowledge. In this regard, we can learn from foreign case teaching method, while allowing more judges, prosecutors and lawyers to do part-time professor at the law school, the system of judicial professional skills and practical skills. In the course of teaching, we should pay special attention to cultivating students' ability to solve problems by

[35] Su [22].

[36] Su [22], p. 306.

using theoretical knowledge. In this regard, we can learn from foreign case teaching method, at the same time, allowing more judges, prosecutors and lawyers to do part-time professor at the law school, and systematically teach professional judicial skills and practical skills.

In 2002, the country held a unified judicial examination for the first time, which improved the access threshold of legal profession and promoted the professional accomplishment of legal professionals. It was a positive reform measure. Unified judicial examination system for legal education can play a "baton" of the guiding and regulatory role, the implicit meaning of the implementation of unified judicial examination lies in establishing the common knowledge background and professional consensus of the legal profession through the access conditions of the legal profession, to create favorable conditions for the formation of professional judicial community.[37] The so-called "judicial professional community" is the abstract community based on common or similar judicial rationality, judicial knowledge, way of thinking and judicial skills, including judges, prosecutors, lawyers, notaries and other legal workers. Unified judicial examination will contribute to the formation of the judicial professional community, the future design of unified judicial examination should be reformed, the focus of the reform is to increase the test on thinking ability, writing ability, problem-solving ability of the examinees, to promote legal education reform, to free education from the established framework, to meet the realistic needs of the times, and this will lay the foundation for future growth of the judiciary!

References

1. Tiechuan H (2004) Random thoughts on the rule of law. China Legal Publishing House, pp 92–93
2. Sophocles (2003) Antigone, translated by Reginald Gibbons and Charles Segel, Oxford University Press, p 73
3. Dingyu Y (2004) Searching for the law. Law Press·China, pp 35–37
4. He Q (2002) The essence of western legal classics. China University of Political Science and Law Press, p 3
5. Bodenheimer E (1981) Jurisprudence: the philosophy and method of the law. Harvard University Press, pp 184–185
6. Xie H (2003) Inquiry of the meanings about law: legal philosophy from the Perspective of Hermeneutics. The Commercial Press, pp 600–601
7. Posner RA (1995) Overcoming law. Harvard University Press, p 57
8. Li L (2001) On good laws. Wuhan University Press, p 283
9. Xie P (2000) Basic legal values. Shandong University Press, p 6
10. Zhang W (2001) Research on the category of legal philosophy. China University of Political Science and Law Press, pp 191–195
11. Pound R (1942) Social control through law. Yale University Press, pp 103–104
12. Miao J (2004) Context and tools: the interpretation of pragmatic jurisprudence. Shandong People's Publishing House, p 30
13. Cardozo BN (1921) The nature of the judicial process. Yale University Press, pp 30–31
14. Liu Z (1999) The theory of legal culture. The Commercial Press, p 67

[37] Liu [23].

15. Fan Z (2001) The coincidence and difference of the Chinese and western legal cultures. China University of Political Science and Law Press. Prefece
16. Fan Z (2001) The basic spirit of Chinese legal tradition. Shandong People's Publishing House, p 333
17. Lin D (2002) Confucian ethics and legal culture: a sociological perspective. China University of Political Science and Law Press, pp 4–10
18. E-xiang W (2004) In: Modern judicial ideas and the reform of trial modes: collection of proceedings of the 16th academic symposium of the national courts. People's Court Press, p 317
19. Zhuru C (2001) The judicial reform and the politics development. China Social Sciences Press, p 8
20. Tianjun K (2005) Law and literature research review, people's court daily, 21 Apr 2005 (B2 edn)
21. Cardozo BN (1931) Law and literature and other and addresses, vol 3, pp 20–21
22. Su L (1996) Nomocracy and its relevant native resource. China University of Political Science and Law Press, p 292
23. Liu J (2003) Enjoy the law: a legal professional's thought note. Law Press·China, p 182

Chapter 3
Quality Constitutions of the Chinese Adjudication Art

The analysis of justice cannot give you a sense of lively sense of justice, as the analysis of jokes will not make you laugh.
—Wu Jingxiong, The Art of Law

The purpose of the realization of the judge's trial is to carry forward the law spirit, to safeguard social fairness, justice and order better, to seek happiness for the whole society. Its content is "true", its essence is "good", its ideal is "beauty", and it is the organic unity of the "truth, goodness and beauty",[1] the art of adjudication puts forward higher-quality request to the occupation judges, only on the basis of meeting the requirements of these qualities, the judges would be able to gradually sublimate their professional techniques and skills to the realm of art.

1 Firm Faith in Law

Rousseau said, "Man is born free, and everywhere he is in chains." This compassionate proverb tells the real, fatal survival of mankind: human beings would never be able to get rid of the shackles of various social relations. The law is the knot of the shackles. From the perspective of human nature, the existence of law is premised on the defects of human nature. People are born with such defects as arbitrariness, greed and selfishness, which cannot be reformed by moral preaching. Instead, they can only be rigidly restrained and disciplined to the maximum extent with the help of institutionalized rational forces such as law,[2] the defects of the law are innate in itself and cannot be eliminated. The ultimate reason for westerners to choose the rule of law, I am afraid that it does not lie in the merits of the law superior to the wisdom of the people, but only to consider the rule of law is more reliable than the rule of man. History also often warns that human self-discipline is not constant.[3] Rule of

[1] Fu [1].
[2] Liu [2].
[3] Liu [3].

Y. Kai, *The Art of Trial Process*,
https://doi.org/10.1007/978-981-15-6434-5_3

law is the ultimate choice of human beings, only the rule of law is the best means of governance. Law is not only a tool to control the society and restrain the citizens, but also to govern the country, to control the government and political parties, and to restrict the behavior of leaders. Therefore, the modern rule of law country is a country that believes in "the supremacy of law".[4] "Law supremacy" is the supremacy of the Constitution and the supremacy of good law, which not only refers to the supremacy of substantive law, but also includes the supremacy of procedural law. The judge firmly believes in the supremacy of the law, delineates the dimensions of the rule of law for the trial of the judge, sets out the boundaries of justice for the exercise of judicial power, and sets the basis for the idea of the art of adjudication.

The law is an important mechanism to regulate the interests and resolve disputes. The judicial model of resorting to court and ruling by a relatively neutral judge has become the most authoritative and conventional means a modern society dispute resolution, and is by far the most peaceful, most civilized and fairest dispute mode in human society, which is recognized as the last defense of social justice.[5] Rule of law as an excellent means of social governance is an indisputable fact. The rule of law society believes in the idea of the supremacy of law, as legal professionals, we should firmly establish the faith of the supremacy of law and the loyalty quality of the profession.

Establish a firm belief in law requires judges to have a correct understanding of the nature and function of law, to have a profound understanding of the spirit of law, and to have a positive expectation of the rule of law. There is a need for a belief that the law is the truth, which is similar to the "dull". There is a need to have a pious faith in law, and lasting love of the legal profession.

The faith has boundless power, and only after the constructing of a firm faith in law, it is possible to love the legal profession and then turn the passion into artistic creation passion and wisdom. Only under the guidance of a firm faith in law, professional judges would continue to pursue the spirit of law, to find the original intention of legislation, to explore the best way to apply the law, so as to transform the professional skills into the art tension.

The firm legal belief is the most basic and essential quality requirement for the judge's trial art. The establishment of a firm legal belief requires the judge to understand the origin and historical evolution of the law, to correctly understand the nature of the law and jurisprudence, to understand the nature and function of the law, to grasp the targeting field of legal norms, to fully master the framework, structure, basic principles and main contents of the major legal systems, to abide by the professional ethics of judges.

Faith is the baton, and faith is the course mark. Whether or not having faith, and the degree of belief determine the behavior of the subject as well as the way, the quality and the real effect of the behavior. Judge in the process of adjudication must continue to cultivate a strong interest in the law, to form the complex of law, to conform to the legal spirit invisibly, to make the advocating of law become the habit and the consciousness. The professional loyalty of the judge comes from the legal

---

[4]Daohui [4].

[5]Liu [2], p. 15.

belief, comes from the deep understanding of the dignity of the judge profession, comes from the persistent pursuit of the just cause, and comes from the courage and ambition of the judge to devote himself/herself to the law.

2 The Legal Professional Ethics and Integrity

The judge's personality is the ultimate guarantee of justice.
—[Austria] Eugen Ehrlich

The beauty of the judge's personality first comes from the moral character of the legal profession. Judges should be moral and profound cultivation of people, and they should always be kindhearted, should be full of sympathy and affection, should keep their fearless and brave, do not curry favour with the dignitary, do not follow the vulgar, taking the law as a guideline and never change. Mountain Tai collapse and stay still, elk beside and not look sideway,[6] the judge is the spokesman for justice, sacred and detached is the essential features. Where does the divine come from? When the judge goes beyond his own interests, when the judge consciously takes the judiciary more important than his own life, when the judge regarded the cause as part of life and let the cause sanctify and perfect the life, the judge would give the sacred feeling.[7] The divine nature of the judge comes from the professional ethics of the judge.

The professional moral quality of judges is very important to the judicial art of judges. Only legal knowledge and judicial skills are difficult to cultivate into art. To achieve the realm of art, the support of legal ethics, skills and ability are required. Therefore, in addition to the accumulation of legal knowledge, judges should pay special attention to the cultivation of noble professional ethics. The jurist Guo Daohui said, to learn to behave as a human being, to cultivate legal ethics, is to learn in a lifetime to be a person who is willing to sacrifice to law. Mr Lu Xun called such person as "the backbone of China". Law should be the embodiment of justice; jurists, legislators, judges, lawyers…… should be the guardian of social justice, the conscience of the times.[8] To cultivate a sense of justice to plead for the people and sacrifice to law, and cultivate the political ethics of "neither riches nor honours can corrupt him; neither poverty nor humbleness can make him swerve from principle; and neither threats nor forces can subdue him", which is to cultivate the people of legal ethics.[9] The professional ethics of judges is the summary of the moral concepts and moral behaviors of judges in the process of judgment. The special status of role and responsibility of judge determines that the judges must have good occupation ethics, the judge's occupation ethics do not only represent the judge's

[6]Lv [5].
[7]Lv [5], p. 475.
[8]Daohui [4] p. 676.
[9]Daohui [4], p. 678.

personal image, but also represents the occupation spirit of the judiciary, conveying the moral concepts and values of the social progress and development. Only when the judges' moral quality and occupation ethics cultivate to perfection, can they in the adjudication process correctly according to the generally accepted moral standards and values to guide the case hearing, to interpret and apply the law correctly, so as to judge impartially, and promote the construction of social equity, justice and order with the perfect moral character and conduct of professional judges. According to the moral quality requirement of judge's occupation, the Supreme People's Court specially formulated "The Basic Rules on Professional Ethics of Judges", the judges' occupation morality standard, put forward strict and clear requirements on the judge's occupation moral. To develop the upright and outspoken occupation ethics, the judge must first learn to resist the temptation and greed. In the current complex social environment, some people may think that money can do whatever they want, and they adhere to the idea of " Money makes the mare go", often use money, sex and other temptations to replace the power of preferential treatment. This is not only a violation of the law, but also an insult to the judge. The court should be the most impartial and incorruptible institution, and all the activities of the people's court must be consistent with the law. Since choosing the legal profession, the judges should be willing to poor, learn to refuse and stand the test of money and sex, take the transformation of the world view as a lifelong training course, firmly establish the moral concept of serving the people and the society's happiness, consciously resist the temptation of money, sex, power, relationships, and friendships, strive to be "noble-minded and pure, a man of moral integrity and above vulgar interests, a man who is of value to the people". There are two ways to cultivate professional ethics: external force, internal self-examination. Among them, the internal self-examination is the most basic method, which requires the judge to set up the warning line for himself, always reflect on the moral integrity of his professional behavior, and promote the on-going improvement of social morality with the upright professional image.

3 Theoretical Knowledge and Experience Accumulation

Specialization of judicial activities is a process of historical evolution. With the continuous development of society, the process of specialization of judicial activities is accelerating, and increasingly, we need a special group of professional judges. Highly specialized and professional judges, not only means the independence and integrity of the judiciary, but also requires the judges to have more than the average person's professional theoretical knowledge structure and experience accumulation, which is the necessary quality requirements in solving the disputes by utilizing the professional techniques and skills within the framework of professional ethics for the judges.

First of all, the judge must have a profound legal theory. The adjudication art requires the judges to have a profound legal theory, because although the judicial trail is a very practical work, the professional requirements of the judicial practice require deep and solid theoretical knowledge structure as the basis of competence. A judge should be a legal expert who has a profound legal theory. The judge's legal theory knowledge structure includes three aspects: one is the jurisprudence and related knowledge. The flashpoint of legal knowledge is jurisprudence, which is the basis of all laws, the foundation of all legal knowledge, and the research method of all legal knowledge. Jurisprudence enables us to know the nature and effect of law, to know what is the spirit of law, what is the rule of law, to understand the nature of the judiciary and the value of judicial procedure, and the relations among law, politics, economy, society, morality, culture, religion, philosophy, art and so on. Jurisprudence is the basic theoretical knowledge of judges in a judicial trial. The second is the specialized legal knowledge, including constitutional law, criminal law, civil law, commercial law, economic law, administrative law, intellectual property law, litigation law, marriage law, inheritance law and other law departments, as well as the related legislative interpretation, judicial interpretation and judicial policy. In recent years, the process of legislation in China has developed rapidly, the judge must continuously strengthen the study, and constantly adjust the knowledge structure of the department law, in order to meet the needs of the development of the times. The third is the interdisciplinary knowledge of law and other subjects and the theory of marginal jurisprudence, including philosophy of law, sociology of law, economics of law, aesthetics of law, literature of law, public relations of law, communication of law, legal culture, etc. In recent years, the interdisciplinary research of law and related subjects is quickly developing, the application scope of these interdisciplinary is very extensive, and the research results are very useful for the judicial practice, which require the judges to learn and master and apply to the judicial practice.

Secondly, in addition to the request for the construction of a reasonable legal theory of knowledge structure, the judge should also learn and master the relevant subject knowledge, because the judge's judicial work is a highly-specialized occupation, involving politics, economy, culture, health, sports, military and other aspects of social life. Today's society has entered the knowledge economy and the information age, with the rapid development of modern science and culture, the knowledge of human being is undergoing the rapid growth of the rate of super-geometric series. In recent decades, the growth of knowledge, far more than the sum of thousands of years of human history, the rapid growth of knowledge led to "knowledge explosion" and "information explosion". The renewal of modern knowledge will be inextricably linked with the legal norms; for example, the rapid development of the internet, has brought a lot of network legal issues need to be resolved. The development of modern science and technology has promoted the birth and development of the new department law, such as intellectual property law, environmental resources law, environmental protection law, space law and so on. The expansion of human knowledge system requires judges to broaden their knowledge and learn more. The art of adjudication puts forward higher demand for the knowledge structure of judges, not only requires judges to have solid legal theory knowledge, but also according to the development of the trial work constantly adjust the relevant knowledge structure, so that their theoretical knowledge structure is not confined to law disciplines, but a wide range of theoretical knowledge structure, requiring judges not only understand the law, but also with their own professional disciplines have a better understanding and timely grasp of the latest developments in various disciplines, so as to improve the ability to solve practical problems.

The legal profession is the profession of experience, and the theoretical knowledge structure required by the art of adjudication should contain the content of the experience. Experience is also a sensible theoretical knowledge, which includes both the experience of the judge's trial and the experience of the social life of the judge. Both are the necessary contents of the judge's judicial art.

4 Legal Thinking Habit and Legal Interpretation Skills

In the process of judicial trial, the judge needs to ascertain the facts and apply the laws in accordance with the legal procedures, which is not only directly related to the litigants' interests distribution, but also the social norms and adjustment. The particularity of the object requires the judge to use the special way of thinking, that is, legal thinking.

Ascertaining the facts and applying the laws are two basic points of the judge's trial. Judges must use legal thinking to ascertain the facts and apply the laws. Legal thinking refers to in the process of justice by means of legal concept, judgment and reasoning methods reflect the understanding process of legal cases, is the use of the abstraction of the legal science and the experience summary to reveal the nature of the matter and to express the cognitive result. Legal thinking is not something mysterious; the judge, after years of experience, accumulated a wealth of legal knowledge and trial experience, would consciously or unconsciously use the method of legal thinking. Even if the judge hasn't received formal, systematic training of legal thinking, this way of thinking can still be produced by judicial practice. The legal nature of legal thinking makes it different from ordinary thinking, and the development of the rule of law civilization even separates the simple legal thinking and precise legal thinking. The art of adjudication we advocate is to master the precise, complete, and normative legal thinking method.

The role of legal thinking is that the judge in accordance with the legal procedures in the process of adjudication strictly adheres to the rules of the law, according to the different characteristics of the different nature cases, pursuing different standards of proof, scientifically ascertaining facts, and explaining and interpreting the law in accordance with the spirit of the law, so as to thoroughly understand and analyze the phenomenon and essence of the case. Legal thinking is the basic quality requirements of the judge's trial, leaving the legal thinking, the judge also lost their own professional characteristics. The judge is not simply and mechanically ascertaining the facts and applying the laws, not condemnation, but a rigorous and prudent rational thinking process, and the crystallization of the wisdom and experience.

The facts ascertaining under the guidance of legal thinking and the truth pursuit in natural science research are different. Natural science insists on eliminating any doubt, requiring extreme consistency and reliability. The legal way of thinking is compounded, not only requires the main bodies to prove "yes", but also requires the obligation subject to prove "no" or unknown "intermediate state".

The application of law is based on the legal order to determine the specific disputes and explain. Jurisprudence refers to the law application as "the application of law" or "the application of legal norms". The process of law application is mainly the process of legal interpretation. The legal interpretation is the core content and basic component of the law application. However, the process of applying the law and the legal explanation in the process are expressed(externalization) by judging reason to be fixed, the judging reason is the carrier of the application of law and legal interpretation,[10] but also the display of judges' legal thinking process. The way that the legal occupation differs from other occupation, is the judge thinking way called the legal thinking, this is the most striking feature of the judge's judicial art from other arts. The art of adjudication is the flower of wisdom of rational thinking and experience.

It is often not easy for the judge to hear the cases and apply the law. The process of applying the law to the judge is often a dilemma or a rack of brains, and sometimes even a little capricious. Judges must use legal thinking to understand the law, explain the law, and this is the art method that judges must cultivate when applying the laws. Whether the judge is fair or not depends on whether the legal thinking mode is correct or not, and the effect of the judgment of the judge depends on the comprehensive application of the legal thinking skills. The legal thinking enables the judge profession to be a profession with rational thinking, the legal interpretation method enables the hearing cases to be the ability of a wise man. Mr. Yang Renshou said that the interpretation of the law can make the law concrete, clear and systematic. Good law is almost abstract principles, and the concept of uncertainty should be specific to maintain the stability of the law; when it is unclear, it is necessary to clarify it and make it clear. Where there is a contradiction or conflict between laws, especially in the interpretation of the way, it is necessary to explain its correct meaning to achieve unity.[11] It can be seen that the guiding ideology of legal interpretation should be based on rational, objective, just and consistent with the purpose of the legislative interpretation of the law to maintain the stability of the law. The legal interpretation should have the characteristics of being appropriate, present, social and creative. The interpretation of law to judges needs to take into account the four characteristics of the legal interpretation, so that the process of legal application becomes the process of legal refinement under the guidance of the legal thinking.

Besides, the judge's trial under the guidance of the legal thinking is not a simple addition of facts and law. In the eyes of the judge, the diversity, the rheology and the concreteness of the legal facts have the natural hostility to the generality, stability and abstract of the law, inner fit is accidental, dislocation is normal. Therefore, the ascertaining of facts and the interpretation and applying of laws are two independent stages of the adjudication, and a process of the inseparable subject and object colliding with each other, which needs to be integrated with special thinking method. Once

[10]Kong [6].

[11]Yang [7].

the judge has a sophisticated legal thinking tool, the adjudication has become a particularly passionate, intelligent and artistic activity.

5 Prudent and Rigorous Working Style

Every profession has its own unique personality, which is the so-called "role theory" of sociology. According to Professor Hao Tiechuan, the judge's occupation personality can be summarized as loneliness, charm, noble.[12] In Cautious Judges and Mercurial Lawyer, Liu Junwu takes the "cautious" as the position of judge profession, believing that Chinese judges, in particular, need to abide by the "cautious" of the professional code of conduct and professional ethics. For the judge, having a wise, sober and rational mind is much more important than the tongue, "I think; therefore, I exist" is considered to be the truth of the judge.[13] The two scholars have different perspectives on the role of judge profession, but both of them have accurately and profoundly summarized the personality characteristics of the judge profession, and position the judge of the professional personality of idealization.

We believe that the professional personality of Chinese judges is "prudent and rigorous", which is the basic quality requirements of judges' professional personality. The charm of judge's profession is derived from the beauty of personality reflected in the legal profession. Judge's judicial art should be reflected in the beauty of judge's professional personality. Therefore, judges must study aesthetics and must study "performing arts". In this sense, the judge is an esthetician and a performing artist.[14] The interpretation of this profession is not an exaggerated, the external drama expression, but the steady, restrained fact restatement; the judge's stage is a solemn court, in this cautious scene there is a mixture of emotions, and there are all joys and sorrows of the world, the judge both in the play and out of the play, both the director and the actor, but at any stage of the repertoire, the judge's character is prudent, rigorous, both cautious in words and cautious in behavior, and its charming features are mature and intellectual.

The judge's professional mission is to make a fair judgment of the case and achieve social justice through rational judgment and careful reasoning. The judicial power is a power to decide, is also a power to judge, judging and reasoning is the important content of the judicial adjudication,[15] The essence of judgment and reasoning is to carefully rule out a possibility or prove a possibility carefully. As the basis of adjudication, judicial judgment and legal reasoning are higher than the general judgment and reasoning. In order to realize the art of adjudication, the judge must get used to the strict legal thinking mode and form a prudent and rigorous work style.

---

[12]Hao [8].
[13]Liu [9].
[14]Hao [8], p. 66.
[15]Liu [9], p. 19.

Careful and rigorous work style embodied as follows: first, the judge should respect the facts, seek truth from facts. Seeking truth from facts means everything must be from reality in the process of the adjudication, respecting the objective facts, ascertain the facts of the original appearance in accordance with legal procedures, thus this fact is the legal sense of the fact that there is legal evidence to prove the objective facts, and not the judge preconceived or to replace the legal truth with subjective imagination, which is the essence of "based on the facts". Careful and rigorous work style is based on objective legal facts, which is the premise of judicial justice.

Secondly, careful and rigorous work style is embodied as the judge's carefulness and rigorousness, that is "restraining in power, restraining in privacy, restraining in speech, restraining in behavior". The acquisition of judicial power comes from the authorization of the people, and the judge must use the judicial power to the people's well-being, and never allow the judicial power to turn into a tool for personal gain. The independence of judicial power requires judges to be "careful", not to conform to the vulgar, not to be involved in the complex secular life circle, and not to be strongly influenced by social emotions. They should maintain prudent professional attitude and behavior habits, and live "alone", this is probably two thousand years ago the great thinkers Lao Tzu said, "leave somebody at large the better to apprehend him", "great wisdom appears dull", "an intelligent man looks dull", "great sound is heard rarely".[16] The exercise of the judicial power requires judges to be restraining in speech and behavior. The judge's speech and deportment is fairness that can be seen by the public. The words and deeds of judges in the process of adjudication are the object of public concern and become one of the criteria to judge whether the adjudication is fair or not. The words and deeds of the judge cannot be because of reckless, irresponsible to make the parties concerned to think that the judge is biased.

Finally, careful and rigorous work style embodied as a fine working attitude of modest, prudent, objective and calm. As an ordinary member of the collective, the judge will also be affected by a variety of emotional factors. In the human society, the judges need to keep calm at all times, to establish a positive and impartial attitude of justice, to treat people and things in fair, not to judge the case with personal likes and dislikes, not to determine the case with personal emotion, not to favor or attack any party with feelings and desires; they must be objective and impartial. The judge must understand that in the course of the case, it is normal that the litigants have emotional opposition and emotional disputes, it is because of the intense conflict of the interests and feelings, the parties concerned would resort to the law in order to solve the dispute. If the judge cannot always maintain an objective and fair, calm, cautious and modest attitude in the vortex of extreme confrontation, the contradiction is not only difficult to resolve, but also may intensify, even confuse the trial.

Therefore, the process of using the legal method of resolving disputes is a process of art. There is a rational legal thinking, a skill of conciliating conflict, experience of running in disputes, a penetrating intuition, skills of figuring out the psychology, eloquence of lecture-field, art of life, which need carefully and strict judicial attitude

[16]Hao [8], p. 65.

as the basis, emphasize the inner thinking and careful solution, and oppose the reckless and assertion of the temperament.

6 Controlling and Decision-Making Ability

The process of litigation is a process of struggle and balance of interests. In this process, there are many unknown uncertainties, sudden problems and the possibility of the intensification of contradictions, which require judges to have strong ability to control and deal with decision-making, Specific performance: the ability to control the whole process of the development trend for the judge, the court trial control ability, the implementation control ability, the mediation control ability, the ability to deal with emergencies, the decision-making ability to resolve the intensification of the contradictions.

In general, the judge can roughly grasp the basic facts of the case, the states of the evidences, the applicable legal provisions and the legal interpretation of the law, but there are always some unknown factors that may affect the case in the course of the trial, such as evidences or evidence clues newly discovered in the litigation process, repeated views of the parties concerned, the new changes of the cases, the emergencies in the trial process of the case, the intensification of conflicts, which require the judge to respond rapidly, to make timely decision and appropriate disposal.

Judge's trial is actually a process of balancing the interests of disputes, in this process, because of the interests of the fierce conflict and strong emotional exclusion, the parties concerned would easily cause trouble, intensify contradictions, and things would get out of control to some degree. For example, the parties concerned may be suddenly faint on the court due to emotional excitement caused by heart disease or cerebral hemorrhage; in the course of the case, the difference between the psychological expectations of the litigation results and the possible outcome of the proceedings, the parties concerned may threaten to take extreme measures to exert pressure; if the verdict fails to meet the requirements, the parties concerned may take revenge on the other party or the judge's way to express dissatisfaction; because the interests involved many aspects, it may lead to large mass conflict events, and so on. The control and response to these unexpected problems is an important part of the art of adjudication. Judges who have many years of practical experience in the judicial trial have their own unique experiences and methods in controlling and responding to the cases. Experienced judges are often able to become frightened, change danger into safety, in response to unexpected events or groups of contradictions intensified disputes like a big general sitting in command of a mighty force, leisurely, be perfectly calm and collected in commanding the army. This is a comprehensive reflection of the judge of the ability to control and decision-making, it shows the judge's smart, clever, bold working ability. The ability of control and decision-making is the synthesis of a series of intelligence factors, such as judge's observation, feeling, thinking, analyzing, dealing with and controlling, and requires the judge in the process of judicial trial to observe carefully, to feel keen, to experience deeply, to think quickly, to analyze accurately, to formulate strategy cleverly, to reply freely. And all the reaction elements must be completed in a specific, limited space-time. We can imagine how difficult it is.

Judge's ability to control first refers to the judge in the course of the case of the overall control and dominance, including the ability to derive the legal procedures, the ability to control the court trial, the guiding and controlling ability to various litigation acts; second is the response ability, that is, the judge in the case of the trial process of intuitive and indirect response ability when facing various new situations or unexpected problems. The judge should have fast reactions, to be able to find the problem and understand the nature of the problem in time, and respond actively; the last is the judge's ability to coordinate, to deal with unexpected problems need to have the coordination ability. For the possible intensification or the intensifying contradictions, the judge can act as a bridge between the two sides to communicate, to conciliate the conflict cleverly and circuitously.

Judge's ability of decision-making refers to: (1) the judge's ability in the trial process of the case, in the face of emergencies to act and make decisions decisively. Sometimes the opportunity to resolve the conflict will be difficult to make up for the loss of missed, and we must take timely measures to deal with it. (2) The judge should have the ability to make a remedy. When the judge discovers procedural errors and misconduct or adverse effects, it is necessary to make clever use of the opportunity to take appropriate measures to remedy and correct.

7 Expression Ability

The judge's legal thinking process needs to be expressed by means of language tools, including verbal explanations, exhortations, persuasion and written instructions, orders, rulings. The judge can only interpret and disseminate the spirit of law by applying the legal norms, adjusting the social behavior and resolving the dispute. The quality of expression depends both on the expression and on the form of expression. The artistic expression of judge trial lies in the judge's judgment is the combination of the two expressions of "verbal and literal", both static words and dynamic speech, is the unity of "form" and "sound", which is different from the "form and color" of painting and sculpture, and "single form" beauty of music and literature. The adjudication art requires professional judges to have both strict, standardized and accurate expression of legal language, but also a clear, concise, vivid oral language expression skills, to expand the tension of the trial art fully.

I. Verbal Expression Ability

Although Mr. Liu Wujun summarized the professional characteristics of the judge to "cautious in words", but here that "cautious in words" is just against "arbitrary speech", "nonsense talk" and "misrepresentation", does not require the judge "talk less", "be silent", or "be afraid to talk". As a social worker, the judge is confronted with the crowd, dealing with the disputes between people, not only through the oral language to express, but also through superb expression and perfect expression. So, "being cautious in words" of judges refers to "being precise in words" and "being kindness in words".

The judge's verbal expression is an important manifestation of the trial activities, through the observation of the judge's words, not only can explore the theoretical foundation of the judge, and even can judge the overall level of the judiciary. As the saying goes, "a word makes one laugh; a word makes one jump." "One kind word can warm three winter months. An acute word cuts deep than a sharp weapon." Good words, can make strange people work together, can make people communicate, can help people solve problems, can make the person entrusted with responsibility. A person who is fastidious about talking art, is often concise and comprehensive; it can improve the social status of the individual to allow for unforeseen circumstances, to accomplish a task with ease.[17] The superb of speaking art is as tuneful as the canary singing, or as bell and drum warning people. The superb of speaking art, every phrase a gem, every word into the bottom of heart, its connotation is rich, full of philosophy, its meaning is profound and thought-provoking.[18] On the contrary, improper words can provoke unexpected calamity, or even make our language building collapse in an instant.[19] The importance of verbal expression is more evident in the field of justice. The process of the judge's trial begins with the hearing, runs under the guidance of speaking, ends by writing, and proceeds by thinking. The guidance of "speaking" determines that the process of adjudication cannot be separated from the art of words, which is the inevitable requirement of the judge profession. First, the court trial requires the judge to control by standard words; second, the method of legal thinking requires the judge to communicate to the parties through the popular words, so as to establish communication platform; third, the spirit of the law requires the judge to express it in a concise, humorous and oral language, laying the foundation for the reasons of the judgments, and preparing for the settlement.

The art of adjudication and the art of speech has a close relationship. The legal text establishes and publics through words, communicates and notifies through the form of language; the legal acts involving words thinking and expression, the legal language is the carrier of the law, the judge's trail is inseparable from the language, and the language of speech is the most direct and the most widely used expression tool. Whether the judge can use the words artfully is of great theoretical and practical significance for the smooth progress of the trial and the effect of the adjudication.

Speech is based on quick thinking and articulate, which requires the corresponding special vocational training. The primary training should be the legal thinking, and the legal language followed. The purpose of training is to enhance the judge's self-confidence, to enhance the expression of language, so that the judge's words become an adjunct to the adjudication. The elements of speech include: in sound, cadenced, sonorous, clear and steady; in meaning, blunt, precise, neutral and without emotion.

---

[17]Chi [10].

[18]Chi [10].

[19]Xiuping [11].

In the training of speech expression, the judges should pay attention to the beauty of the language, the harmony and beauty of the sound and the beauty of the meaning, the beauty of the form and the beauty of the content, and learn the different characteristics of the different stages of the litigation, to distinguish different connotations of the beauty of words, to utilize different speech techniques.

In addition to verbal expression ability, judges should also learn how to use body language expression. The so-called body language refers to the external expression of the body through the expression of the will of the people, is a non-word language means of the transmission of information, including human movements, gestures, posture and expression, etc. Body language can play a complementary role in language.[20] The public social judges, whether a judge can judge the case fairly, the judge's body language is one of the important aspects. Imagine that if the judge in the process of adjudication to convey the body language is absent-minded, anxiety, recklessness and arrogance, or hesitant panic, drowsy difficulties, and even shows as discriminate on one side or both parties, even if the judge is strictly in accordance with legal procedures in the adjudication, the parties concerned would have reasonable doubts about judicial justice. Therefore, body language is another form of verbal language, also has the characteristics of intuition, identification and expression. The correct body language can reduce the doubts of the parties concerned and the public about the impartiality of the judge, helping to reshape the image of the judge, especially the fragile judicial authority.

II. Literal Expression Ability

The expression of words is a professional skill that judges often use in the process of judgment. The judge's trial requires the production or examination and issuance of a variety of judicial documents, including judgments, conciliations, verdicts, judicial proposals, notifications, notices, etc. The process of making judicial documents is the process of using words to express will. It is of great theoretical and practical significance for judges to complete the tasks artistically whether the judge can skillfully use the ability of expression. The judge's most important expression ability is writing of judgment documents. The judgment document is the carrier of justice, is the window to show the judicial system and legal culture of a country. The United States Justice Gray said, "The judge's decision is the law." The judge must have the strong ability of literal expression, especially the reasoning part of the judgment documents. Good judgment documents should be able to make the parties both clearly aware of the reasons for the winning or losing of the lawsuit, so that the winning party to win clearly, and the losing party to lose clearly. The French writer Beaumarchais said in his book *The Marriage of Figaro*, "The judge who refuses to explain the reasons is the great enemy of the law." Indeed, with the requirements of the rule of law, the judge must explain the reasons in the judgments, refusing to explaining the reason is the enemy of the application of law.[21] Only to clearly tell the judging reason, the

[20]Zhao [12].

[21]Kong [6], p. 37.

parties concerned would be convinced, the judgment would have credible and moral persuasion, and to make the rule of law to carry forward.[22] So, how to tell the reason? First of all, the reasoning is not simply answering questions, reasoning is not solving a complex problem. Judge instruments focusing on controversy as the core of the argument, the argument should be comprehensive and not cumbersome, flat and not thin, professional and not shy. The knowledge of jurisprudence and the skills of legal science prepare the materials for judgment and reasoning. Judges should use the text ability to screen, organize materials, arrange the overall structure of the argument, so as to be simple and appropriate, both to avoid duplication, but also to prevent omission. This is the first step in literal expression. Secondly, the judge uses the literal expression to fill the content of reasoning. The judgment documents are characterized by accuracy, preciseness, conciseness, stability and strict programming. The literal text of the expression of the contents of the instrument should correspond to the special writing requirements beyond the general political writing rules. It should have the basic characteristics of the general political writing: normative, rigorous, to avoid the discourse and descriptive words of strong subjective colors and the lyric and evaluated words of strong literary colors. This requires the judge to have a profound knowledge of the Chinese language skills and the ability to control the language, and through repeated consideration, modification of the judgment documents text to make the judgment documents to be grammatical, clear and coherent, explicit.

8 The Ability to Understand Human Nature

People living in the real society, must have connections with others, the judge is no exception, must deal with the parties concerned and the various people in society, so that proper handling of interpersonal relationships is the basic quality of the judge's trial.

As mentioned above, it is an art of behaving oneself. Judges are always in the process of getting along with people, often dealing with complex relationships. Dealing with interpersonal relationships is even more challenging than applying the laws at some point. Some judges may be able to deal with the problem of "matter", but unable to deal with the problem of "human", and it is precise because the "human" problem is not handled well, it will affect the social effects of the adjudication. In the objects of judge's trial work, there are people of good character, and persons of bad character; there are people of stable emotion, and people of heavy emotion; there are good people, and there are bad people; there are ordinary people, and there are rich and powerful people; there are sensible persons, and there are unreasonable persons; there are people of no relationship with the judge, and there are students, friends, colleagues, relatives and other related concerns; there are people who understand the laws, and there are people who are legally blind, or who are not completely

[22] Kong [6], p. 37.

understood. All of these require the judge to treat and educate equally with a fair and just heart. In the process of handling a case, if the judge masters the skills and methods of doing things, he would be able to handle and deal with the complex interpersonal relationships involved in the case, so that it is the cases' justice, but not the interpersonal relationship which determines the cases' trail. Judges who are well versed in people are often very popular with the parties concerned, the opposing parties are very easy to mediate and reach an agreement, or even the case is decided by verdict, the two sides would also accept it, no dispute exist anymore; on the contrary, the judges often make the relationship very tense, not only the two sides are at daggers, but also the relationship between the parties and the judge and the court is also very tense, and the contradictions are easily intensified. In particular, the first instance of the basic level, originally a straightforward dispute, if the judge handled improperly, it would easily make the contradiction expanded and complicated.

China is a human society, in the Confucian tradition of the mainline of history, the custom of emphasizing human relations has become the mainstream of society, the fixed idea in people's thinking is: the law is nothing more than human relations. The concept of humanity has been deeply rooted in people's minds. Therefore, China's judicial trial should also be based on the reality of Chinese society and integrate more humane legal ideas and methods, in accordance with legal procedures and the spirit of the law, paying attention to the proper handling of interpersonal relationships. It is an important professional skill and method of judges on practicing the humanistic view of law to pay attention to the philosophy of life in job-related performance of the individual and group of judges. A judge in the practice of judicial trial more from the perspective of human nature to achieve the humanistic care of the law, isn't it a manifestation of human beauty? The law in provisions becomes warmth, living law by the judge of the professional skills in the use the legal concept of humane, isn't it a wonderful art?

References

1. Fu Q (1996) The art of handling cases of the lawyer. Law Press·China, p 26
2. Liu J (2003) Enjoy the law: a legal professional's thought note. Law Press·China, p 13
3. Liu X (2003) West window & law rain. Law Press·China, p 6
4. Daohui G Challenges of the times of law. Hunan People's Publishing House, p 545
5. Lv S (2004) The truth, goodness and beauty of law: primary exploration of legal aesthetics. Law Press·China, p 473
6. Kong X (2004) The method of legal interpretation and case study. People's Court Press, p 35
7. Yang R (1999) Methodology of jurisprudence. China University of Political Science and Law Press, pp 96–97
8. Hao T (2003) Law is an art of living. Law Press·China, pp 10–22
9. Liu J (2003) Enjoy the law: a legal professional's thought note. Law Press·China, pp 19–22
10. Chi L (2004) On speaking art. China Public Interest Press, p 1
11. Xiuping A (2005) Course on judicial eloquence, China University of Political Science and Law Press, p 3
12. Zhao X (2003) The framework of chinese judge system: some problems on the professional construction of judges. People's Court Press, p 262

Chapter 4
The Evaluation Standard of the Art of Adjudication

The difference between the legal artists and the legal technician is the emotion, or as Cardozo said, "a mood as the acme of perfection, a desire for delicate and noble"
—Wu Jingxiong, The Art of Law

Any professional skills will have different levels, and there are evaluation and measurement standards, the art of adjudication is even so as a superb judicial professional skill. I think that the following aspects should be taken into consideration in the evaluation standard of the judge's judicial art. First, the judge's trial is to practice the spirit of law and the value of the system pursued by law, the degree of realization of the value of the system of law is the basic criterion for evaluating judges, and this is the starting point of the study of evaluation standards for the adjudication art. Secondly, the judge's trial is a kind of social activity, the judge's trial mode should have a fine social basis, the results of the adjudication should have a fine social effect, and the judge should have a pure and fine social image. Thirdly, since the judge's trial has the influence of the existence and the foresight of development, it requires reform spirit, to pursue the survival of the future and positive. The evaluation standard of the judge's art should be universal and long-term, and it will not lose its practical significance.

Based on the above considerations, we believe that establishing the evaluation criteria of the judge's judicial art should start with the value of the judge, that is, the social value and the legal value of the judge's trial. Leave the value system of the judge's trial, and any evaluation criteria are unscientific. Based on this, we confirm the evaluation criteria of the art of adjudication as: the truth of the adjudication, the goodness of the adjudication, the beauty of the adjudication, as well as the value of happiness contained in it, which is the abstract integration of the legal value system.

The existence and development of all things contain the contradiction of the unity of opposites. The unfolding of the contradiction is to start from the positive to the negative, and then to the negation of negation, that is, "theme, antitheses, synthesis". The existence and development of law is also the same. As a basic and systematic part of the superstructure of society, the three-dimensional structure of "theme, antitheses, synthesis" constitutes the framework of "truth, goodness and beauty". Law is the product of social civilization, and along with the development of civilization. From

Y. Kai, *The Art of Trial Process*,
https://doi.org/10.1007/978-981-15-6434-5_4

the overall trend, the higher the level of social civilization, the more truth, goodness and beauty in the law. The law of truly complete and closely integrated of truth, goodness and beauty is the most ideal law.[1] Similarly, when the judge's trial realizes the truth, goodness and beauty of law, and the spirit of law is practiced, so political civilization reach the realm of art, thus truth, goodness and beauty is no longer the purpose of the trial art, but the trial art itself.

1 The Truth of the Art of Adjudication

First of all, to explore the truth of the art of adjudication, it is necessary to analyze and demonstrate the true value of the law, only to understand the value of the law's truth can clarify the truth of the art of adjudication.

Montesquieu in his masterpiece "The Spirit of Laws" identified the truth of law as, "Laws are the necessary relations arising from the nature of things."[2] "The necessary relations" is the regularity, the truth of law is the essential attribute of law, that is the regularity of law. Hagel, in his book "Elements of the Philosophy of Right" with profound dialectics conceived a set of strict operating rules of the law mechanisms (abstract law—ethics—ethical law).[3] Marx also made a brilliant exposition of the truth of law, "The legislator, however, should regard himself as a naturalist. He does not make the laws, and he does not invent them. He only formulates them, expressing in conscious, positive laws the inner laws of spiritual relations."[4] "The truth, is the regularity of the object things of their own reflected from the world movement, changes and development."[5] That is to say, the truth is the regularity of the existence and development of things. "Truth" refers to the attainment of truth and the attainment of the state of truth, that is, the necessity for the subject to fully approach and fit the object in thought and action.[6]

Throughout the above discussion and understanding the truth of law, we believe that the truth of law should be understood and grasped from the regularity and the purpose of law. First of all, to consider "the truth of law" from the perspective of three-dimensional structure is the natural conclusion of the regularity of law and the purpose of law; secondly, from the perspective of philosophy of law, the truth of law essentially expresses the law as the truth of the provisions and stability, reliability. This is from the legal philosophy to think about the true value of law, put forward

[1]Lv [1], p. 1.

[2]Baron de Montesquieu, The Spirit of Laws, The Online Library of Liberty, p. 30.

[3]Lv [2], p. 2.

[4]Karl Marx Frederich Engels Collected Works, Volume 1 Marks:1835-1843, Lawrence & Wishart Electric Book, 2010, p. 308.

[5]Wang [3], p. 32.

[6]Ii [4], p. 373.

the truth is an important form of the value of the law and the rule of law, so as to give us some new thoughts on the value of law.[7]

Among the truth, goodness and beauty of law, the truth of law is the basis of the goodness of law and the beauty of law, the foundation of the order of fair and justice, the morality of the judge's professional skills, the origin of the judge's conscience, and the root of wisdom that can lead the judge to the truth. As professor Fan Zhongxin said in his book "Law is Truth", we take law as truth, and we dedicate our whole life to practice and guard the law's "truth".[8] The truth of law requires the judge in the judicial process to find, to pursue, to practice, the pursuit of the truth of the judge trial art means that the judge in the trial of case to pursue the regularity and consciousness of law, to fully reflect the truth-value of law through judicial activities. If the rule of law to come true, there is a need for thousands of people to believe that law is truth; if the art of adjudication to come true, there is a need for the professional judges to regard the belief that law is the truth as the eternal values of the profession. Only our professional judges group first set up the faith and ideas of law is truth, can they lead the masses who yearn for the ideal of the rule of law to the road of finding the goodness, the beauty and the happiness.

The truth of law pursued by the art of adjudication does not mean the legitimacy, justice and truth of the abstract legal entirety. The truth of law has its concrete connotation, including the truth of the legal norms, the truth of the legal facts, the truth of the legal procedure, the truth of the legal conclusion, and the truth of the judge's expression.

The truth of the legal norms first refers to the formulation, modification and abrogation of the law must follow the real needs of social reality, in line with the economic development and the progress of civilization of the overall society, with the basis of natural generation and the possibility of appropriate transcendence, reflecting the inevitability and regularity of development as a whole. The second is that, when applying the law, the judge can solve the legal truth, to fill the legal loopholes, to relieve law incompetence, to practice legal value, and not to misunderstand nor omit the law.

The truth of the legal facts means the legal facts, the foundation of judge's trial, are objective, evidence-supported, not speculative or fictitious. The truth of legal facts is different from the truth of objective facts. The truth of the legal facts emphasizes the relativity, the proof, the rationality and the validity of the method of proof, and the truth of the objective facts pursues the absoluteness, the consistency and the scientific nature of the means of proof.

The truth of the legal procedure is that the design of the procedure should conform to the dual value of substantive justice and procedural fairness, which is in line with the cost of social and economic conditions, guarantees both fairness and efficiency. Meanwhile, the truth of the legal procedure means that the judge strictly complies with the requirements of the proceedings, does not sacrifice the procedure for the entity, nor distort the procedure for the local convenience. The judgment documents

---

[7]Lv [5], p. 72.

[8]Fan [6], p. 2.

correctly record the execution of the procedure and the legal consequences of the procedure.

The truth of the legal conclusion means that the judge's trial is based on legal facts, taking the legal norms as the yardstick, the legal procedure as the basis, the legal value as the core, through rigorous thinking and prudent judgment, to exclude discrimination and prejudice, to constantly get close to individual justice and social justice of the judgment conclusion.

The truth of the judge's expression means that the judge in the decision-making process to express their views on the facts of the case; for the understanding of the law and the evaluation of the relevance and correspondence between facts and laws, the judge dares to adhere to the principle, and the correct views, should not be guided by the might or influenced by the public opinion, should have the ability to propose the solution and the courage to undertake the responsibility.

2 The Goodness of the Art of Adjudication

If the good is defined as the positive value of morality or utility, then the goodness of law is the positive value constructed on the basis of the truth of law pursued by the law. The subjectivized objective necessity of law and the subjective imagination given to it together constitute the positive value of the goodness of law. The goodness of law has various forms of expression and realization, generally including justice, fairness, equality, freedom, rights or human rights, democracy, rule of law, power, order, safety, effectiveness or efficiency.[9] It is also the embodiment of values of justice, freedom, democracy, order and efficiency. The goodness of the art of adjudication, that is, the judge in the process of adjudication to explore and pursue the appropriate behavior and just result on the basis of the truth of the art of adjudication, and the basic value system to realize the good law: justice, freedom, democracy, order and benefit.

The goodness of law performs as, the objective, external and empirical law which is the law in the true sense transforms into the subjective, internal and metaphysical law, law of conformity transforms into law of purpose and ideal, law is posse transforms into law in esse, so as to directly inspire people's subjective initiative and the normative role of human behavior. From the truth of law to the goodness of law, is the first negation or self-sublation of law, is a great progress of law itself.[10] The goodness of law is the evolution on the foundation of the truth of law, from the truth of law to the goodness of law is a leap in the spirit of law and the value of legal truth. If the goodness of humanity as the sunlight can disperse the hearts of the haze, the goodness of law is such dawn, spread the various values protected by law to people's full of contradictions and disputes hearts, not only to exclude the wonders but also unlock the knots.

[9]Lv [7], p. 267.
[10]Lv [8], p. 268.

The goodness of law includes both the personal good protected by law, that is all good wishes of individuals to pursue within the scope of the law, includes a variety of public purpose pursued by law, and also includes a variety of utilitarian values, such as property interests, personal interests and public welfare, even more includes the ethical values maintained and promoted by law, such as honesty, kindness, loyalty and equal care etc. Justice is not only suitable for the goodness of law, but also the goodness with most legal nature in all goodness.[11] Justice is the most important value in the legal value theory, is the most basic value of human pursuit and ideals, since the birth of human society, justice has become a noble pursuit in the moral, emotional and awareness for human, the goodness of law should first be the goodness of righteousness. Justice theory is the evaluation criteria that can reflect the social public good feelings. When we evaluate the goodness of the art of adjudication, we should take justice as the primary value, how to correctly judge the standard of justice is an important content of the judge's judicial art. The process of judging a case by a judge should be a process of realizing social justice through legal professional techniques and skills. The outcome of each case's judgment should reflect the pursuit of justice and seek the maximum welfare of the greatest majority with the justice in law.

The values of legal freedom are based on the basic meaning of freedom, and at the same time combined with the legal requirements of the law, to protect the freedom of the people recognized by society, whereas to limit people's infinite freedom by law. Judge's judgments of the standards of legal freedom in the process of the adjudication (that is, judgment on the reasons why law allows and limits the freedom of people) is the artistic trade-off. The judging criteria for legal freedom are not in the law itself and require judges to explore the causes of freedom and the degree of freedom from complex social life. From the complex social life to find the evaluation criteria of the legal freedom is the righteousness of the judge's professional skills. Judges should seek the standard legal freedom from the material and spiritual level, especially carry out the judicial work from the purpose of good law, avoid evil, defend and develop the freedom of the individua, promote people's sense of a utonomy to a certain extent through a high level of judicial trial, expand the behavior scope of the people, complete the constitutional and legal mandate given to the judges.

In the modern sense, democracy refers to a system of people's autonomy, a kind of social self-management system, an ideal pursuit of political life and social life. The emergence and implementation of legal rules are closely related to democratic values. Only democratic society can produce democratic legal rules; the legal system is closely linked with the concept of democracy, and the legal system continues to develop because of the constant pursuit of democracy. The realization and guarantee of democracy is the basic task of law. Democracy is the prerequisite and foundation of the rule of law. The upbringing of democratic thought can promote the awareness of people's rights and strengthen the concept of freedom, and help to cultivate the law-abiding spirit of social mass. Law is the main carrier and expression form of the democratic system, which can standardize and materialize the contents of the

[11]Chengliang [9], p. 107.

democratic system. The legal principle is the basic criterion of democratic activities and can make up for the inherent defects of democracy. The ideal pursuing democracy in mankind needs to be run on the track of law laying, and the judge's trial is to correct the deviation from the orbit and protect the good behavior and self-care mechanism of goodness. Safeguarding democracy is one of the values that instruct judges to practice trial. Whether judges have the concept of democracy of modern society and whether to pursue the best effect of handling the case in democratic values is the embodiment of the art of judicial trial.

The order we discuss is the legal order, is a rule-regulated social order, the people's legislation is to use the power of law to adjust the various social relations, to maintain a stable and orderly good state. People want to live in a safe society, where the good order makes people have a desire of goodness, and the desire of goodness inspires the harmonious humane atmosphere, the good humanities environment causes the human to create the fervor which creates and the artistic desire. It is through the way of judicial trial, the judge, on the one hand to build the normative order in the law, on the one hand to help establish the friendly customs on the moral, to practice the rule of law the good people yearn for, in order to achieve the law control of social order. In this sense, the level of the art of adjudication is closely related to the degree of judicial control of the social order.

The benefit was originally a concept of economics, with the in-depth research of the relations between law and economy and the development of the science of economic analysis law, the concept of benefit breaks the barriers of traditional jurisprudence, and becomes a kind of value in the field of law. As a form of social control, no matter what specific purpose the law needs to achieve, it hopes the process and results of its regulation is effective, one of the purposes of law is to make the object adjusted and the career promoted reach an effective operation.[12] Justice delayer is justice denied. The judgments of no benefit is not justice, but the waste of judicial resources and the loss of the parties' interests, not to mention it's not the realm of the art of adjudication. From the perspective of economic efficiency, the judge trial should pay attention to the efficiency, the significance of the efficiency makes "justice and efficiency" become a parallel theme of the court work. The benefit view of the judicial art, refers to in the judicial practice, the judge through continuously improve occupation skills and master the common characteristics of cases and the rules of procedure development, without prejudice to the judicial quality, continuously improve the efficiency of the trial work, so as to achieve the purpose of law. Studying on the benefit value of judge art, its purpose is to analyse the benefit of the judicial trial, to constantly sum up the application of skills and techniques, to maximize judicial efficiency and the conservation of judicial resources and litigation costs.

The judge's judicial art pursues the goodness of law which combines the above various legal values, which means not only the law itself is the good law supported by the valuable system, but also the humanization of the judicial process and the

[12]Lv [10], p. 373.

personification of the judicial behavior.It refers not only to the reasonableness of the law, but also to the good nature, morality and justice, virtuous and dignified behavior.

3 The Beauty of the Art of Adjudication

An animal forms things in accordance with the standard and the need of the species to which it belongs, while man knows how to produce in accordance with the standard of every species, and knows how to apply everywhere the inherent standard to the object. Man therefore also forms things in accordance with the laws of beauty.

—Karl Marx, Economic and Philosophic Manuscripts of 1844

Beauty is a fascinating topic with a long history.

The meaning of beauty is very rich, covering almost all aspects of social life. The beauty of the judge's art is to explore the essence of the judge's art from the perspective of aesthetic stereoscopic consciousness, the relationship between subject and object, the combination of sociality and objectivity. From the perspective of aesthetic stereoscopic consciousness, the beautiful thing is not the beauty itself, but emotion in the heart of a person who appreciates beauty. Different minds would feel different beauty, and one mind facing the same thing would have a different understanding of beauty in a different space-time. People may have a basic understanding of the beauty of something, but they never get an "understanding smile" in the face of something, which means that the beauty is the result of mutual feelings of the subject and object. Sometimes the subjective likes and dislikes would cover up the objective form, but the long-term practice and sensory evolution, combined with the social persuasion, make people to have a true relative evaluation of the objective existence.

For the professional techniques and skills of the judge's trial, the authorities or bystanders will have their own feelings and experiences. In the judicial practice, we often hear the litigants or the audience to attend and observe the trial to evaluate a judge of high level of trial, a judge dealing with the problem cleverly, a judge writing judgments wonderfully, it is actually people's naive feeling of the beauty of the adjudication art. The beauty of the judge's art exists in the three-dimensional consciousness of the people, which is the subjective feeling that different people produce when they witness the professional skills of the judge. From the perspective of the relationship between subject and object, when the judge's superb techniques and skills showed in the trial process fit the evaluation standard of beauty in the subjective consciousness of the public and litigant parties, when the two blend into one, it becomes the art of beauty. From the perspective of the combination of sociality and objectivity, the aesthetic standard of the judge's judicial art is manifested in the practice of judgment. The perfect combination of the beauty of reality and the beauty of imagination is the essence of beauty. Law aesthetics is an emerging marginal discipline, which is a combination of law and aesthetics. Judge trial art has become an important research content of aesthetics.

In people's minds, law has rational, conservative and realistic character, while beauty has a sensible, free and romantic character. How the two seemingly different things together and formed a new subject? There are historical and realistic reasons. In the study of aesthetics, estheticians initially research in the beauty of the field art, then began to study the natural beauty and social beauty, more just focused on the beauty's figurativeness and emotionality, while ignoring the beauty's abstractness and reason. Modern aesthetics has extended the field of research to all aspects of social life, trying to explore the aesthetic world of the whole human society, scholars through the study have recognized that the definition of human beauty is too narrow, leading to the narrowness of the aesthetic research. People began to identify that emotion and reason, image and abstract, are not diametrically opposed, but dialectical unity of mutual inclusion, mutual integration and mutual transformation. Therefore, the scope of aesthetic research is expanding, and there are more and more interdisciplinary research fields, such as technical aesthetics, scientific aesthetics and legal aesthetics. Plato, the ancient Greek philosopher, first put forward the question of "what is beauty", he put forward the theory of "beauty is idea" and "the beauty of law" from the standpoint of idealism. In his view, "the legal justice is a kind of order, is to have their own things, to do their own things." At the same time, "when the three qualities of the individual (desire, passion, and reason) are in good order, the individual becomes a just man."[13] Aristotle believed that harmony is necessary for beauty, harmony is beauty, explicitly argued that "it is more choice-worthy to have law rule than any one of the citizens",[14] the purpose of city-state and law is to promote the just, and the true meaning of law is "to make the citizens good and just".[15] Gustav Radbruch, a contemporary German legal thinker, political activist and humanist, holds that art and poetry can help the legal profession to reach the highest level, and clearly puts forward the establishment of aesthetics of law.[16] The proposition and construction of aesthetics of law provide more aesthetic theoretical support for the research of the art of adjudication.

Chinese traditional culture attaches great importance to the aesthetic temperament and character, as one of the traditional legal culture also attaches great importance to the integration of aesthetics and law. In the history of five thousand years of civilization in China, the perception of beauty is closely linked with politics and law. Represented by the Confucian, the Confucianism advocated the rule of man, rule of virtue and rule of Li, highly appreciated the value of art in human life and political order, emphasizing the consistency of artistic beauty and political domination in social purposes, and advocating the close combination of windy beauty and concrete rituals. Taoism emphasized the beauty of legal connotation, to take the highest moral and state of law as beauty. Today, China takes the construction of a rule of law

[13]Lv [11], p. 401.

[14]Aristotle, Politics, translated with introduction and notes by C.D.C. Reeve, Hackett Publishing Company, 1998, pp. 96–97.

[15]Aristotle, Politics, translated with introduction and notes by C.D.C. Reeve, Hackett Publishing Company, 1998, p. 80.

[16]Lv [12], p. 403.

society, a harmonious society as the ideal, not only insisting on the rule of law, but also encouraging the people to pursue the perfect life through self-improvement. The perfect life needs the esthetic realm, and the harmonious society also needs the rule of law environment to promote the esthetic education. Therefore, the construction of aesthetics of law in contemporary China is not abrupt, instead, it is inevitable.

The difference of the characters of law and beauty, rationality and sensibility, reality and romance, conservatism and freedom, is actually only the differences in their respective characteristics and forms. It seems that there is no connection between the two, but there is a natural symbiotic nature of the relationship with each other and mutual penetration relationship. Only the fusion and penetration is not as obvious as other forms of art, nor as rich in expression as in other forms of art, so that it is not fully observed and understood. However, the relationship between law and beauty is objective.

The beauty of the judge's trial art is the most closely connected with the judicial practice in the research of aesthetics of law. The law is the carrier of human reason, through the provisions of the rights and obligations to express rational and abstract requirements; at the same time, the law also accumulates human emotions, it is expressed in different ways, showing the image that can be perceived, whereas the art of adjudication is the best way to express human feelings by law. The judge's trial art makes the integration of reason and sensibility, abstract and image in law to the realm of beauty. By injecting the aesthetic taste and artistic vitality into the judge's occupation skills, it is able to rise the judge profession into the aesthetic dimension, to help the professional judge group to find the value basis of individual development accurately in the judicial practice, so as to realize the harmony between individual ideal and social responsibility.

The meaning of exploring the beauty of the art of adjudication is to explore the ideal and practical tasks of the judges' career, to explore the ways of improving the vocational skills. The construction of aesthetics of law is the inevitable requirement of the nature of law and the development of the times, and to carry out the aesthetic study of the art of adjudication is the inevitable requirement of the construction of judges work team and the development of the professionalization and superiorization of the judges group. The beauty of the art of adjudication includes judge's beauty of posture, beauty of words, beauty of temperament, court's beauty of clean, beauty of solemn, beauty of stateliness, court trial's beauty of order, beauty of rhythem, beauty of standardization, judgment's beauty of words, beauty of jurisprudence, beauty of proof, etc. The judicial acts, the judicial process, or the judicial atmosphere, anything that can lead the audience to generate admiration, conviction, identity and other feelings on the law, the rule of law and the judicial procedure, can be recognized to has an artistic beauty.

How can we turn the beauty of the judge's judicial art from a deliberate act into a conscious act? The answer is still to follow the rules of beauty, to judge according to the law. Follow the rules of beauty to construct the occupation skill, is to reflect the human nature of law and the spirit of law in the practice of judicial trial, so that the law truly becomes the law that embodies the needs of human nature, rather than the tool of domination and despotism; to make justice a bridge for the people to enjoy the beauty of law, rather than a place people feel the evil of law. This is the basic idea of advocating and evaluating the art of adjudication!

4 The Art of Adjudication: The Art of Truth, Goodness, and Beauty

Only when the unity of the truth, goodness and beauty of law is the perfect state of the harmony of feeling and reason, harmonious, and complete happiness. And only in the realm of beauty can we achieve the social responsibility and historical responsibility of the judges' profession, realize the professional value of the judge and the full value of the law.

As an empirical form and value form containing truth and overtop truth, containing goodness and overtop goodness, the beauty can make the truth and the goodness of the judicial trial to be more fully reflected. Beauty and truth and goodness are the unity, and the professional skills that are in accordance with the rules of beauty are often true and good. When we judge the professional techniques and skills of judges by the standards of beauty, the judicial trail becomes a true art.

At the present stage, the judge's judicial art is not high and the aesthetic feeling is insufficient, often because of the separation of rational thinking and perceptual thinking, abstract thinking and image thinking. Only with the rational thinking, the abstract judgment and the reasoning, neglecting the unity of truth, goodness and beauty, the judge can just be a mechanical and indifference law craftspeople, by no means an artist. In the modern sense, the judge should have both aesthetic consciousness and the ability to comprehend beauty, so as to handle the cases within the natural law, ethics, emotions and moral, to deal with all kinds of contradictions and disputes, to enjoy the joy and pleasure of the occupation under the rules of beauty, and to fully show the gentle and upright human nature through their judicial practice.

Beauty is the speech of happiness, the thing that makes people happy. Aristotle believed that happiness is not quality, but the "good", arising in accordance with virtues, which is the activity of the soul, the activity that has been chosen for its own sake. He put the rational contemplation attributed to happiness, and believed that the contemplation is the good and the perfect happiness, "Happiness, then, extends as far as contemplation, and the more contemplation there is in one's life, the happier one is."[17] We agree that the process of contemplation is the process of happiness, but also believe that the significance of legal thinking is more than that. In addition to the sense of happiness of the main body of speculation, the results of legal reasoning can also lead to the formation of the sense of happiness of the speculative object, which is a multidimensional experience of happiness. Meanwhile, we agree that happiness is the natural reaction in accordance with virtues, but the virtues are not natural and universal. The power of virtues lies in practice, the beauty of contemplation is also derived from practice. The judge profession is a profession which is always

[17] [Ancient Greek] Aristotle, Nicomachean Ethics, Cambridge University Press, 2004, p. 198.

practicing, and full of speculation. The judge's speculation and practice constitute the overall of the art of adjudication, and constitute the source of the happiness of judicial objects.

The happiness value of law is the fruit of the truth, goodness, and beauty of the judicature, is the highest realm of the art of adjudication!

References

1. Lv S (2004) The truth, goodness and beauty of law: primary exploration of legal aesthetics. Law Press·China, p. 1
2. Lv S (2004) The truth, goodness and beauty of law: primary exploration of legal aesthetics. Law Press·China, p. 2
3. Wang C (1981) Aesthetics illuminated. People's Publishing House, p 32
4. Ii X (1995) The principle of dialectical materialism and historical materialism. China Renmin University Press, p 373
5. Lv S (2004) The truth, goodness and beauty of law: primary exploration of legal aesthetics. Law Press·China, p 72
6. Fan Z (2000) Law is truth. China Legal Publishing House, p 2
7. Lv S (2004) The truth, goodness and beauty of law: primary exploration of legal aesthetics. Law Press·China, p 267
8. Lv S (2004) The truth, goodness and beauty of law: primary exploration of legal aesthetics. Law Press·China, p 268
9. Chengliang Z (2002) Justice in law. Law Press China, p 107
10. Lv S (2004) The truth, goodness and beauty of law: primary exploration of legal aesthetics. Law Press·China, p 373
11. Lv S (2004) The truth, goodness and beauty of law: primary exploration of legal aesthetics. Law Press·China, p 401
12. Lv S (2004) The truth, goodness and beauty of law: primary exploration of legal aesthetics. Law Press·China, p 403

Chapter 5
Principles of the Art of Adjudication

> *When we realize that our life is a dream, this is the most real moment of our lives, because we realize that we are dreaming, isn't it more than the dream itself closer to the situation?*
> —Wu Jingxiong, The Art of Law

We say that the art of adjudication has the composition of emotional thinking, it doesn't mean that judges can do whatever they want based on feelings and intuitions. On the contrary, the art of adjudication must follow certain principles and norms. The so-called principles are the corresponding codes of conduct formulated in accordance with the law of development of things. The principles of the art of adjudication is the basic guiding rules of the judge trial developed on the basis of the judge's professional characteristics and rules and the objective requirements of the art of adjudication.

1 Combination of Rigorousness and Flexibility

Judges must be strictly in accordance with the provisions of the law, which is the bottom line of the principle of the judge's trial, is an insurmountable gap. "Basing on facts and taking law as the criterion" is the basic principle of the art of adjudication. Rigorousness refers to the judge's trial must be in accordance with the spirits and principles of the rule of law, all professional techniques and skills should be found in accordance with jurisprudence, and then there is "reasonable" problem. Adhere to the spirit of the law and the principle of the rule of law requires the judge to resist the temptation of power and money, put aside all kinds of human relationships and selfish desires, to achieve fair justice and impartial judgment. However, the rigorousness requirement is not isolated, static, must be combined with flexibility, the two are the dialectical relationship of dialectical unity. Only combining the rigorousness and the flexibility, the judicial art is an organic whole. If there is only rigorousness but no flexibility, or there is only flexibility but no rigorousness, there would be no existent and development space for the judicial art. It is often said that, "the law is dead and human is alive", "the law is nothing more than human relations", it is actually the

Y. Kai, *The Art of Trial Process*,
https://doi.org/10.1007/978-981-15-6434-5_5

dialectical unity of rigorousness and flexibility and the creative combination of the two in the judicial practice.

The combination of rigorousness and flexibility has three meanings:

First of all, insisting on the rigorousness is the basis of the judge's judicial art. The cultivation of art should have a clear scope and characteristics, the scope of the judge trial art should be the judgments, and the judgments have strict procedural requirements and law-applying requirements. All flexibility is based on the rigorousness, leaving the rigorousness, the flexibility would lose the support and value of the existence.

Secondly, flexibility is a useful aid to the principle, the basic principle is universal, in solving the specific problems of the case, it would require the flexibility to play a complementary role. The complementary role of the flexibility is guided by the basic principles of the judicial art, and the judges do not judge the case deviate from the acting mode determined by the basic principles and has a relatively broad discretion space to consider the special situation. In handling different cases, the judge should abide by the principles, and according to persons, affairs and local situations, flexibly grasp the characteristics of the case, pay attention to the details of the case, to avoid compliance of the principles mechanically.

Finally, the utilization of flexibility requires the judge to have the spirit of innovation. The flexible judgment of the judge should not be enslaved to the existing models. The intention of flexibility is to encourage judges to be sensitive to the new problems in the face of strange cases, daring to think, and put forward a variety of options that can be applied, from which choosing the most appropriate solution. Meanwhile, flexibility is not a free state of simple disorder, and the spirit of innovation is not blind unconventional. The innovation spirit under flexibility means scientific innovation, rational innovation, cost economic innovation, and the innovation that can afford the strict scrutiny of the rule of law on the foundation of basic principles.

2 Combination of Theory and Practice

All the research fields of social science emphasize the combination of theory and practice. The combination of theory and practice is both the scientific research method and the correct thinking route. The process of the combination of theory and practice is that people are taking the practical need as the starting point for research, with profound theory as the research tool, with practical experience to enrich the theoretical accomplishment, with the theoretical attainment to design the system in accordance with the practical need, with the system operation results to verify the scientific theory and promote the development of the theory, so as to serve the new need of the practice. This is a process of continuous connection, continuous conflict, continuous division and continuous approach, full of struggle, but towards unity.

The judicial trial is the special social activity, and the main field of the effect of jurisprudence as well. The judge's trial is the important form of the judicature, is one of the ways of exercising state power, but also a platform for the protection of individual rights. It is a continuous developing, continuous trying out and comprehensive coordination behavior system, including multiple levels, requiring the system executor, the judge, to perform the duties almost perfectly. The specific form for the judge to perform his duties is the unity of the subjective and objective, and the unity of subjective and objective is the combination of theory and practice. The combination of the theory and practice of the judge's trial includes two meanings: first, the judge's legal theory combined with the practical experience, the theory and experience as the mutual inspection and complement for each other, together play a role in the process of adjudication; second, the legal theory system confront with the examination of the facts, the theory develops with the development of practice, the rule of law goes to reality through the optimized theory, and the rule of law realistic experience constantly test the existing legal knowledge system of the judge.

The art of adjudication asks the judge to pay attention to the study of the application law, improve the artistic content of the practice, and constantly enrich the accumulation of theory, and be good at connecting the renewal of theory and the change of reality, pay attention to the practicality of the theory, at the meantime pay attention to the diversity of the actual needs, regulating the practical reasoning with the theory, stimulating the vitality of the theory with the practice, so that the combination of theory and practice is not only the principle of the art of adjudication, but also becomes the habit of the judge's behavior.

3 Combination of Law and Society

The art of adjudication has both legal and social characteristics: on the one hand, the judge's judicial trial is the responsibility of the Constitution and the law, the judge must perform the duties within the jurisdiction in accordance with law and in accordance with the legal procedure. The judge's decision must be the result of the proper application of the law, and the legal nature is the basic characteristic of the art of adjudication. On the other hand, the trial practice of judges is the practice in society, which is an unusually active legal practice that is closely related to the public. The goal of the trial work is to achieve the social expectations of natural justice, rather than a privileged class design of the pretense of the fair. Only when the legal sociality of the judge's trial incorporates into the sociality can the law realize its value. Left the soil of social life, and then the laws can only be castles in the air. Only the close combination of law and society can help to achieve the social function of the law.

The law arises from the practical needs of social life. For the relationship between the legal rules and the social life structure, "the Social Rules of Dualism" Hayek expressed the following idea: although people cannot prove that the social order naturally produces its internal rules, that the order of things is inherently rooted in the nature of the human being, but people cannot infer that the rules that guide people's behavior must be generated by selection and design, cannot be inferred that people through the choosing rules to shape the community. Hayek's view actually implicitly reveals the objective process of the social life on raising the law, and at the same time, does not deny the human subjectivity and the rule's independent character, thus creating an important path for us to understand the relationship between law and society.

In 1959, the International Commission of Jurists took place in New Delhi, India. The New Delhi Congress discussed the theme of "the rule of law in a free society". In its conclusions, the committee on the legislative stated that under the rule of law, the legislature carried out the function of creating and maintaining conditions that would uphold the dignity of man. This would include recognition of civil and political rights as well as the establishment of the social, economic, educational and cultural conditions, which the committee deemed essential to the full development of the individual's personality. Legal norms are necessary conditions for the implementation of the rule of law, and the rule of law takes legal norms as a tool to adjust social order, the purpose of law is to achieve a civilized state of civil society. Today, the legal norms are increasingly understood as universal social rules, with its purpose is to restrain the state power to support the socio-economic development, "standard of right" has given place to "standard of obligation". The trend of social life is more restrictive limiting the creation and change of law than ever before, and is more dependent on legal attitudes and actions than ever before.

The cognition and judgment of the status or essence of judicature in the social structure involves the semantic understanding of "judicature" and is also the cornerstone of the whole judicial theory. As a political phenomenon of the whole political society, the abstraction of the essence of judicature can only be obtained by resorting to its most common structural position in society, in order to get a scientific explanation.[1] The reason of emphasizing on the combination of law and society of the art of adjudication is based on the structural status of judicature in society. First, from a historical point of view, judicature is a structural element in the political system that is prevalent in political society. Since human beings entered civilized society, the judiciary has been stable existed. The earliest king was the earliest judge. The development of human society is synchronous with judicial structural development. With the development of the society, the more complex the social relationship, the stronger the society's demand for judicial function and the dependence on the judicial structure.[2] Secondly, the art of adjudication occupies a very important position in the judicial structure, and is the connection between the judicial structure and the society. The judicature is the constitution of social order, and the art of adjudication is the composition of the civilized judiciary, the judge's professional behavior influences the behavior of social members by acting on the object of the adjudication, so as to influence the social practice of the mass. The level of judge's occupation skills directly determines the precision degree of the judicial effect. Finally, the judge interprets fairness through the art of adjudication, and expands the tension of the judicature to social order. The role of judicature in the social order is not limited

[1]Zhuru [1], p. 16.

[2]Zhuru [2], p.18.

to passive recovery, and is not limited on compensation and comfort to the weak in society. On the contrary, the judicature is a kind of positive and sometimes aggressive force, which tends to change the social structure, expand the social relations and adjust the social imbalance. This kind of dynamic role of judicature depicts another side of the combination principle of law and society.

References

1. Zhuru C (2001) The judicial reform and the politics development. China Social Sciences Press, p 16
2. Zhuru C (2001) The judicial reform and the politics development. China Social Sciences Press, p 18

Chapter 6
Nourishment of the Art of Adjudication

The most beautiful thing we can experience is the mysterious. It is the source of all true art and science.
—[American] Einstein
In the art of law, judges should be the artists to interpret. The real law cannot be found in the books of the Codex and the law, but in the interpretation of the judge, because as music is not something on the music book, the law is not something in the book.
—Wu Jingxiong, The Art of Law

The art of adjudication is difficult to find in the books, often gives people a feeling of mysterious, so people will be regarded as the technique of "being perceived rather than expressed". Newly appointed judges would often feel it unattainable at first. In fact, where is a certain degree of difficulty and conditional restriction in grasping the art of adjudication, it is not something that is unpredictable and is not a book without words, but a professional technique and skill that can be perceived and expressed, which is a professional skill that can be trained and cultivated. The art of adjudication is explored, researched and refined in the judicial practice by the people, the normal people engaged in judicial trial, but no one takes it as a science to study. With the art of adjudication, there are many experience composition and ideological perception, with a strong subjectivity and individuality, which makes people feel strong mysterious. However, as long as exploring hard in practice, constantly summarizing, supplemented by the correct way and method, each newly appointed judge can continue to strengthen the artistic level of adjudication in the professional career. We firmly believe that, after long-term study and thinking, the newly appointed judge would reach handy, ease, and freely harmonious realm of the adjudication art, and becomes a true jurist and artist.

1 Persisting the Professional Education of Judges

Legal profession requires a high level of judge's education, and requires practitioners to develop the lifelong learning habit. College education only lays the theoretical foundation for the future judicial practice for judges, the follow-up education and

Y. Kai, *The Art of Trial Process*,
https://doi.org/10.1007/978-981-15-6434-5_6

study should run through the whole occupation career of judges. The follow-up education includes two forms, the training education and autonomous learning, in which autonomous learning is the main way of the follow-up education for judges.

I. The purpose of follow-up education

The priority of follow-up education is to define the purpose of the education.

The Judges Law prescribes that those who can be appointed as judges are law graduates or non-law profession graduates with legal knowledge and passed the Nation Bar Examination, have a certain legal knowledge before serving as a judge. But only by the legal knowledge of the pre-vocational college education, it is difficult for the judge to deal with the ever-change realistic questions, not to mention to achieve the artistic realm of adjudication. In civil law countries, the judges have to go through 1–2 years of specialized legal professional skills training before appointed as a judge, while currently Chinese judges are lack of this training process before the appointment, often after the judicial examination and a short-term training then would be appointed as a judge. At present, the judge qualification training period is different in different provinces, some is one week, some is half a month, the longest is no more than one month, there is no uniform vocational skills training materials, there is no professional teachers, usually in the vicinity of colleges and universities to hire a number of temporary teachers to teach, and invite some senior judges of practical experience as well. As the purpose of training is not clear, the corresponding teacher matching, course content arrangements, time configuration is neither uniform nor reasonable, which directly affects the effectiveness of education and training.

Many judges do not have clear purpose in autonomous learning, do not know what the problem is and do not know what is the occupation requirements; there is no learning plan, lack of pertinence, often only to deal with the newly introduced laws and regulations, but can not understand the legal spirit and the implied direction of the rule of law. Therefore, whether it is training education or autonomous learning, we should first know what our purpose is.

The purpose of follow-up education for judges is different from that of the college education for students of law school. It should take the improvement of judicial ability as the core, supplemented by the renewal of knowledge structure and the judicial ideas, at the same time paying attention to improve professional ethics, so as to achieve the art of adjudication.

II. The contents of follow-up education

The contents of follow-up education are as follows:

1. Broadening the legal knowledge to solve the problem of narrow knowledge of judges. With the development of social life and times, the legal knowledge structure is also constantly updated, and college knowledge always falls behind the needs of practical development. At present, the curriculum of law school in China has not yet included the professional judicial skills, not to mention the

art of adjudication. There is a big gap between the students' knowledge, skills and experience acquired during law school and the requirement of the practical work; the major in law and the judicial practice do not necessarily fully fit, the new situation, new problems and the interaction role with other disciplines faced in the trial practice, all these make the knowledge of the newly appointed judge seem relatively narrow.

2. Renewing the knowledge structure to solve the lagging problem of legal knowledge. With the rapid development of legal research, part of the legal knowledge of the newly appointed judge learned in law school would inevitably become old and outdated, lagging behind the needs of the times; with the legislation speeding up, the cycle of the enactment, amendment and repeal of the law is shortened, the original studied law may have been replaced by new legislation, which requires judges to "upgrade" through follow-up education, in order to keep up with the pace of development.
3. Strengthening the training and learning of vocational skills, to solve the vacancy and lack of professional skills, to improve judicial capacity. As mentioned earlier, at present, the pre-vocational professional technique knowledge of the newly appointed judge is basically blank. Aiming at this problem, the judge training institutions and individual judges should focus on the cultivation of judicial capacity, the way of cultivation is to practice, the process of cultivation is to accumulate, the method of cultivation is to learn from experience.
4. Strengthening the knowledge of cross disciplines and related disciplines, to make up for the lack of other professional knowledge of judges. The field of knowledge involved in modern justice is more and more extensive, not only a lot of legal knowledge, but also more involved in other disciplines. For example, intellectual property trials involve a large number of patents, trademarks, copyrights, networks and related natural sciences, and modern criminal trials often involve medicine, psychology, physiology, sociology, and ethics. With the development of society, the modern judicial trial involves more and more extensive industry and fields, and the knowledge of interdisciplinary and related disciplines is more and more demanding, which puts forward higher requirements for judges' follow-up education.
5. Strengthening the study of jurisprudence, to solve the problem of renewing the knowledge of judges' jurisprudence. Jurisprudence is the real glittering point in law, and jurisprudence is not only the foundation of all legal knowledge, but also the forefront of the development of all legal knowledge. Without the support of jurisprudence, it is difficult to open up a broader space for any department law. Meanwhile, the knowledge of jurisprudence is the theoretical support of the art of adjudication. The judge's professional skill is based on the deep understanding of jurisprudence. A judge who does not understand the knowledge of jurisprudence and does not know how to utilize the knowledge of jurisprudence to solve specific problems, is certainly a judge who does not know the art of adjudication. Therefore, jurisprudence is also the glittering point of the art of adjudication. Without the understanding, grasp, application and updating of the jurisprudence, the art of adjudication would be cast into the shade.

III. The method of follow-up education

The purpose is to guide the content and method, the content is to reflect the purpose and determine the method, and the method is to carry the content so as to achieve the purpose. The method is the foothold of the social science research.

The improvement of the professional skills of the judges requires the accumulation of long-term practical experience and the follow-up study of knowledge. With the accumulation of judges' trial experience and the growth of social experience, and through continuous learning, the judges would continue to enhance the judging level. In the follow-up education and learning, paying attention to learning method would get twice the result with half the effort.

1. Establishing the focus of follow-up education
   The judges should establish the learning focus according to the work needs of the judicial trial and their own characteristics, especially to adjust the scope of study constantly according to the basic requirements of the judges' professional skills, the trend of the development of the rule of law, the degree of individual accumulation, and covering the corresponding knowledge points and the width of knowledge according to their own shortcomings and deficiencies. In addition, a major characteristic of follow-up education is to get rid of abstract and macroscopic, emphasizing positive and pertinence, so the judge set the focus on the arrangement and learning must be closely linked with the judicial practice, with practical function, but taboo the inclination of the legalism of "emphasis on text and neglect of idea".
2. Making full use of various ways and channels to carry out follow-up education
   It is not enough to improve the professional skills of judges only by one way of learning methods and ways. The art of adjudication is a comprehensive occupation skill, is the integration of the judges' multidisciplinary knowledge, practical experience, social experience and individual wisdom, a single learning method and way can not meet the need of artistic accomplishment, so that the judges should take more ways to attain more knowledge. It is necessary to pay attention to the study of theory knowledge, but also pay attention to the accumulation of practical experience; it is necessary to pay attention to grasp the spirit of law from the law books, but also pay attention to the broader knowledge elements from newspapers, journals and the Internet; it is necessary to pay attention to the experience in cases, but also to participate actively in the academic discussion and experience exchange activities; it is necessary to pay attention to learn from the experience of senior judges in the trial process, but also pay attention to learn from the experts and scholars; it is necessary to pay attention to systematic learning, but also pay attention to immediate, short-term training. Taking a variety of channels and ways of three-dimensional learning would help judges to broaden their horizons, knowledge accumulation, to ensure the learning and improvement based on the judicial effectiveness.

2 Cautiously Observing the Legal Existence

Observing is the direct way to improve the art of adjudication, and the observing ability is one of the basic qualities of the judge's trial. The ability of observation is the ability of judges to use their senses to perceive and absorb all kinds of information in the course of the adjudication and the ability to extract them into the objective reference of the adjudication.

The contents of the observation are relatively extensive, and there are different focus in the different stages of the adjudication: the first is the observation before the court trial. Before the court trial, the judge should observe and acquaintance with the basic situation of the litigants (third party), entrusted agent, legal representative and their basic views on the case; especially for the case of a certain social impact, the judge should also observe the views and opinions of the public on the nature and the handling of the case, so as to take corresponding measures and methods in the court trial. The second is the observation in the court trial. The court trial is the important part of the adjudication, and also a place to show the judge's judicial art. The internal needs of the parties concerned, the views of the case, the degree of urgency of the dispute, the emotional fluctuations, the signs of intensification of contradictions would be shown in the court trial. As long as cultivating the habit of careful observation, the judge would be able to detect the developing trend of the case in the courtroom, so as to accurately grasp the proceedings of the case. The third is the observation during the trying process. The judge in the whole process of the case should develop a keen observation habits, to understand and grasp the related information and the perplexing relationship of the case at any time, to understand the objective environment changes and the impact of public opinion, to seize the best time to deal with the case. If there is a possibility of mediation, it can be done timely; if there is an intensification of contradiction, it can be disposed in time to avoid the expansion of contradiction. The fourth is the observation of the case after the conclusion. The judge should sum up experience and lessons, listen to the views of the parties concerned and the public on the results of the case, to know the legal effect and social effect of the adjudication. The fifth is to pay attention to the observation of other judge's judicial skills, to learn from the experience of peers. The sixth is to observe in daily life, to accumulate more social life experience.

The judge's habit of careful observation should be made from the following four aspects: the first is to observe carefully, to carefully observe all the links and the contents of the above six aspects, to avoid inadvertent omission of any minor information, "knowing oneself and one's enemy ensuring the victory". Only carefully observing and timely grasping of all the circumstances involved, the judge can grasp the initiative of the case trying. The second is to observe comprehensively. The judge should understand and grasp the full details of the case, but also observe the various circumstances of the case, including the policy, social environment, folk customs, and so on, and doesn't listen to only one side or interpret it out of context. The third is to observe accurately. The judge should have the dialectical observation ability through the phenomenon, and be good at removing the false reality, stripping out the legal case with the legal significance from a large number of facts. The fourth is to observe fast. Many of the situations in the judicial process would change rapidly, and some small but significant phenomena are fleeting, which requires judges to have very quick dynamic observation capabilities to capture and analyze the phenomena in a timely manner.

3 Paying Attention to the Strength of Judicial Practice

Practice is the fundamental way to improve the level of the art of adjudication. The judge must master the art of adjudication to learn, to observe, to experience and to percept in the rich judicial practice.

Firstly, the judge should actively participate in judicial practice. The judge's occupation is a kind of practical work, and it is necessary to accumulate the practical experience of the adjudication. The judge should actively and boldly handle various types of cases in judicial practice, or attend and observe in the court trials, reading files and the judgment documents to accumulate the relevant judicial experience from the sideway. By the meantime, although the judicial division of labor is growing finer and finer, the judge engaged in the trial work is often confined to a certain type of case, the judge should be a professional as well as a generalist. Different types of cases have similarities, the method and skill of the adjudication are of consistency, and the different places can complement and learn with each other.

Secondly, the judge should be good at summing up the experience of the trial, which is also a learning process. This way of learning cannot be replaced by the college education, is the necessary way to improve the art of adjudication. The judge cannot handle the case on the case, lest nothing after the adjudication, but to learn to sum up the experience of success and the lessons of failure, to refine the regularity, so as to guide the future practice. There are four main ways to conclude the trial practice: first is to insist on writing a diary of judicial work, which is a good way to accumulate work experience. In the judicial process, the judge can write down the bit of experience and sentiment, problems encountered and the solutions, thinking ways, the judicial thinking, the application of legal questions and so on. To review every day's trial experience, days and months multiplying, the art of adjudication will improve. The second is to insist on writing the case reports. The case report is a document that must be attached to the case, which is a kind of judicial document that every judge must write. However, some judges do not pay attention to writing the case report, simply because the case report is asked to attach to the volume, and taking the case report for dual purpose, thus it is both the case report and the judgment document, failing to take the case report as the summary of the trial experience. I believe, whether it is a judgment or mediation, or a withdrawing case, it is necessary to write a case report. The characteristics of the case, the specific analyzing method of the case, the success experience and lessons of the case, the reasons for the success or unsuccessful mediation, the experience and opinion of the application of law, the situation of the court trial, the investigation of the public response, the personal experience and feelings of handling the case and other contents should be summed up into the case report, and every case becomes the material of experience and the ladder to enhance the ability. The third is to carry out research actively. In a sense, the judge's ability of investigation shows the level of the art of adjudication. The novel, major, complex, and difficult cases and the common problems of a certain kind of cases, all these can be carried out the research in a timely manner, to seek the rules through the rise of contention. The fourth is to compare. In the process of adjudication, the judge should learn to use the method of comparison to sum up and improve the level of the art of adjudication, at any time to compare the current judicial method with his/her own experience and other's experience, to compare the ways of the applicable law and the relevant policy, to rethink and review, to learn from those people with good qualities, to introspect from those people with bad qualities, not only to enrich the experience, but also enrich the personality.

Postscript

29 years of judge career, I have experienced too much, people, events and cases, all these have gradually changed my understanding and attitude of the society and human nature. Many things I used to care about so much, now have been past. For the persons I ever loved, appreciated, disliked, hated, I also gradually forgot the memories of the love and hate, and returned to the calm years. And once the suffering overtime work of the trial business research in the Research Office has inadvertently evolved into the indispensable way of life and career realm…

With the growth of age, the perseverance of the law and judicial research continues to increase. It seems that I can never forget the passionate and roseate dream when I initially entered the profession. I'm not sure this passion came from the understanding of the truth, goodness and beauty, or from the mysterious fantasy of happiness, but there is a real understanding of the existence: there is not much belong to us in the world, and there is no "eternity" at all. I always have the passion and impulsion to think, always have the joy and sorrow to contemplate, always questioning about the problems of the meaning and methods, and always wandering in the edge of the pain of knowing and unknowing, and tasted the feeling of loneliness…Perhaps, independent thinking is a happy experience, and willing to be lonely is a romantic feeling? More "serious" is that the state of pondering has gradually become my normal life, I have been accustomed to this living and surviving way, and I feel satisfied, relieved and full of happiness.

The art of adjudication is the question that I have been paying attention to and thinking about in the judicial trial work for almost thirty years. From entering the profession, I began to observe, study and think with the strong interest in the art of adjudication. The whole process of my judge career is the record and writing process of this book. Thanks to the experience of judicial practice in the intermediate and grass-roots courts, both in the trial department and research office, I have the different perspectives to see the research value and practical rationality of the art of adjudication. Thanks to Center for Rule of Law Strategy Studies, East China

Y. Kai, *The Art of Trial Process*,
https://doi.org/10.1007/978-981-15-6434-5

University of Political Science and Law for giving me a great platform to develop my legal research career. Thanks to Central China Normal University, for sincerely giving me an opportunity to start my career as a legal scholar. The experts, professors of law school, with their academic theory of law, deep exquisite teaching art and professional dedication, made me benefit greatly and contributed to my career transition from court to law school.

I would like to thank Mr. Li Long, my PhD supervisor, a senior professor of Wuhan University School of Law, he gave academic guidance to the theoretical construction of the study of the sub-project from the perspective of jurisprudence and sociology of law. I would like to thank professor Cai Hong of Zhongnan University of Economics and Law School of Law, she gave academic guidance to the theoretical framework and development of the study of the sub-project from the perspective of civil procedure law. Scholars' deep concern about judicial practice profoundly inspired my professional dedication as a quota judge, and their intellectuals deepened my understanding of practical rationality and made the subject have more connotations. The research of the subject has also been supported by many other professors, judges and lawyers, and here I would like to express my gratitude! In the future, I will be more diligent in writing to return to the savior in my life and the judge peers to sincerely support me in my judge and professor career.

Kai Yang
June 17th, 2020.

The manufacturer's authorised representative in the EU is Springer Nature Customer Service Centre GmbH, Europaplatz 3, 69115 Heidelberg, Germany. If you have any concerns regarding our products, please contact ProductSafety@springernature.com

Printed and bound by CPI Group (UK) Ltd, Croydon, CR0 4YY
30/09/2026
02225513-0001